Group Time

Resources for Teaching Around the Circle

by Ellen Booth Church

Illustrations: James Hale

Copyright © 1997 by Scholastic Inc.
All rights reserved. Published by Scholastic Inc.
Printed in the U.S.A.
ISBN 0-590-06253-0

1 2 3 4 5 6 7 8 9 10   02 01 00 99 98 97

Contents

Introduction:
A Circle of Children

"Rashad, come sit next to me!"

"Here's a place for you, Jesse."

"Can we sit together for circle time?"

Children are gathering for group time and the excitement of forming the circle is heard in their comments. Something magical happens at group time … children join their energies and create a feeling of community, collective learning, and sharing. Circle time gives children the opportunity to come together as individuals and as a group.

The Circle: A Symbol of Community

Throughout history, the circle has been used by many cultures as a place to share ideas through conversation, demonstration, dance, and song. No wonder then, that circle time has traditionally been the starting place for the young child's day in the classroom. This place of shared community and learning prepares children to spend the day together in a variety of small and large group activities.

Circle Time:
A Place for Sharing

Why is circle time such an important part of early childhood classrooms? As children share information about themselves and listen to others sharing, they become aware of their individuality and of their membership in the group. They develop self-esteem and start to work cooperatively with others. They learn that they won't always get a turn when they want it and that they can't always sit next to the teacher or a special friend.

Circle Time:
A Place for Learning

Circle time gives you and children the opportunity to plan curriculum while you interact as a group. It is also the place and time for children to learn more about their own and others' cultures. They experience the joy of singing and dancing together, of sharing feelings and making new discoveries. The enchantment of a story transports the group to new lands and shared experiences.

The Importance of
Group Collaboration

At circle time, children can investigate cognitive activities together. As you introduce new themes, children learn to help plan curriculum, record ideas, explore language and literacy, and investigate and discuss math and science concepts.

Most important, group time is where children know they will be listened to when they express their ideas and feelings. Their creativity and self-esteem blossom in a safe environment where they feel free to speak without fear of making mistakes.

Whether you're working with preschool or kindergarten children, circle time can be a place of shared joy for everyone. Take your cues from children. Listen, observe, and show them that group time is where everybody counts. You'll be continuing a time-honored tradition.

Group Time Guidelines

Pre-Kindergarten

■ provide a few short small-group meetings instead of expecting all children to come to the same group meeting each day.

■ create interesting and exciting circle times that mix dynamic activities (songs, fingerplays, movement, exercise) with more quiet listening activities (stories, flannel board, experience charts).

■ clearly and simply state expectations, directions, and group time rules. Use positive reinforcement of appropriate behaviors to guide their interactions.

■ select stories, songs, dances, and poetry that invite children to repeat a line, phrase, sound, or motion.

■ encourage children to take turns sharing experiences. Taking turns and listening to each other is a learned behavior that can take preschoolers the entire year to develop.

Kindergarten

■ provide a supportive environment for children to express their feelings and a meeting structure in which every child has a chance to be heard.

■ offer many occasions for brainstorming — ask open-ended questions.

■ expand group time to include more shared reading and writing activities.

■ ask children to suggest topics to study or questions to investigate.

■ invite children to lead group time, giving them a chance to guide discussions or brainstorming ideas.

■ suggest that children work out interpersonal conflicts themselves. First, present the problem, then ask them to suggest ways to resolve it and to vote on different methods. Later they can discuss the outcome.

Time

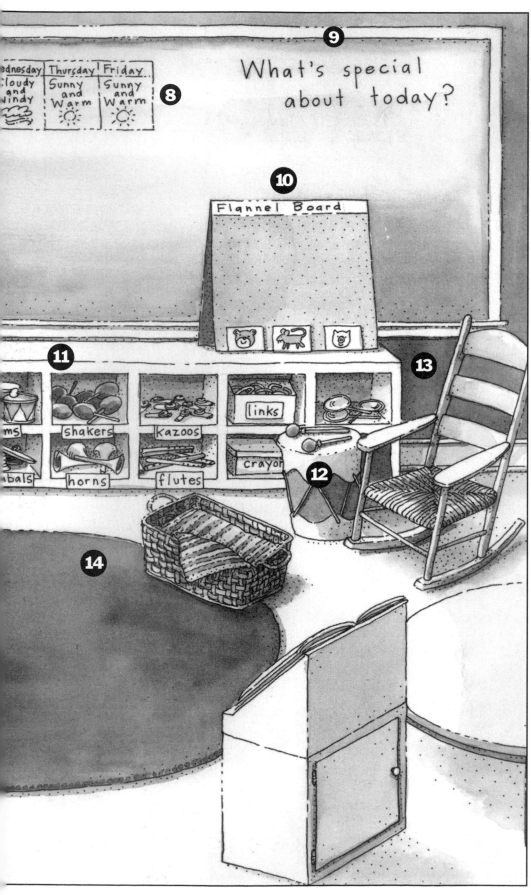

1 "How Tall Are We?" chart invites children to think about themselves in relation to the group and to represent growth in a graphic form.

2 Sharing a poem helps children explore rhyming and wordplay.

3 A tape recorder enables you to record group songs and stories and take down brainstorming sessions.

4 Puppets may help some children express their feelings to the group.

5 A variety of wordless and homemade books encourages children to make connections between the written and spoken word.

6 "Our Classroom News" chart invites group members to share and discuss meaningful experiences.

7 An open-ended question can spark group science explorations.

8 A weather chart encourages children to discuss natural events and learn temporal terms.

9 "What's special about today?" This question boosts descriptive language skills and encourages children to share feelings with the group.

10 A flannel storyboard invites children to sequence events and to create new stories together.

11 A variety of materials support children's explorations. Labels encourage reading, sorting, and classifying skills at cleanup time.

12 A drum is handy to use as a signal for children.

13 A rocker or armchair makes the teacher seem more accessible and adds a homelike quality to gatherings.

14 A comfortable, cozy rug and mats make the circle a clearly defined and nurturing place.

Your Place in the Circle

Speaker • Listener • Performer • Participant • Inspirer • Questioner • Leader • Follower •

Your role in group time is multifaceted and multidimensional. Sometimes you provide information and instruction for children. At other times you lead a song or game or introduce new materials. You listen and follow the children's lead — and all of this can happen in one 20-minute session! Here are a few ways you can ensure that you support children during group time:

Plan and practice.
Gather all your materials and props ahead of time, rehearse reading a selected book, decide how to demonstrate new materials or sing a song, think through what you want to accomplish — and then be ready to abandon the whole plan if you need to!

Set clear limits, rules, and expectations.
Everything from the importance of taking turns to the meaning of "sitting on your bottom" needs to be defined and demonstrated. Invite children to help you make and set group time rules.

Watch, listen, and evaluate.
When you take your cues from the moods and interests of children, you can be certain that you are providing a group time that fits their needs.

Model good listening, speaking, reading, and writing behaviors.
Children are great imitators, so demonstrate the variety of literacy experiences you want them to develop.

Create a safe environment.
Help children understand that they will not be judged, even when they express their thoughts and feelings.

Stretch children's minds.
Use group time as an opportunity to ask questions and expand children's problem-solving, creative, and critical-thinking skills. Children can learn a great deal from listening to one another's strategies for solving problems.

Celebrate diversity.
Ask families to share their knowledge, culture, and interests with the group. Acknowledge individual children, as well as the group, by supporting their unique styles of communication. Your positive reinforcement during group time will build children's self-esteem all day and throughout the year.

Admit mistakes.
Nothing liberates a group more than finding out that teachers make mistakes too. Ask children to help you when you can't remember something or when you fill out the weather calendar wrong. They love showing YOU what to do!

LEARNING & GROWING
With Group Time

Through consciously engaging children's minds and hearts,
we begin to help children become an active community of learners.
The roles you and your children play
at group time can set the stage for all their learning.

Sharing, Showing & Teaching

nticipation fills the air as the children assemble. They are excitedly clutching their cherished possessions and projects as they gather in a circle. The diversity of the children's experiences and recordings promises that an interesting group time is ahead!

A Share Circle

A share circle offers children the opportunity to tell their classmates what they did and learned during a project. For instance, children can share discoveries made while building creative constructions, such as different ways to create shelters or the best way to erect a bridge across the block area.

Making Sharing Work

Just as with any group meeting time, this time needs to be organized. Here are a few tips:

■ **Tell children what to expect** in advance. Children need time to organize and prepare their presentations.

■ **Ask a child to state the "rules of order."** This will remind the other children to pay attention, to respect and celebrate each other's creations, and to offer constructive suggestions.

■ **Keep things moving.** Encourage children to be brief, out of respect for others who also need time to share.

■ **Vary the location.** Sometimes you will need to meet in different areas of the room so that children can see firsthand what others are doing.

A Learning Circle

Share circle is an empowering experience for children. As they report on their projects, they become the researchers, demonstrators, and teachers — and they take their responsibilities very seriously! Not surprisingly, children tend to work with extra care and interest on projects they know they will be sharing with others.

In share circle, children's attention spans increase. These times give children an opportunity to verbalize information, present ideas, report findings, and use higher-order thinking skills, including assimilating, synthesizing, analyzing, and evaluating. The sense of community created in share circle means that children are rarely bored.

What and When to Share

Graphs and charts are excellent vehicles for presenting project findings. For example, children investigating light — and wondering which objects light will shine through — can present a picture graph of their predictions and findings in share circle. (In fact, you may want to keep some graph forms available for children to use on their own.) Other items to share include children's journal writing, stories, letters, science field books, games, songs, plays, puppet shows, and video- and audiocassettes.

Of course, sharing takes place in many settings informally throughout the day. But the more structured share circle can take place at the end of workshop or learning-center time, when children are excited about what they have just done. In addition to showing completed work, share circle can be used to discuss works-in-progress and to invite children to help one another answer questions or solve problems they are having with their projects. By encouraging children to problem-solve, think, and work together, you are fostering curiosity and resourcefulness and creating a community of active, cooperative learners.

A New Twist to Show-and-Tell

The original intent of show-and-tell was to provide opportunities for children to share things from home and to use expressive language as they talked to the group. During each session, a few children would take turns sharing and discussing objects they had brought from home. The teacher would ask

Letting Children Lead

When children take the lead, you can have even more meaningful group times and also build self-esteem. Why not invite children to take turns being you during real group time meetings? Just keep these things in mind:

■ **Be sensitive to children** who don't want to take on the role of leader. Find other ways they can contribute.

■ **Invite children to lead** a small portion of group time at first. Start with a song or the calendar.

■ **Allow children to experiment** with doing things their own way.

■ **Give undivided attention** to the child leading.

■ **Invite children to discuss** how it feels to be in charge.

open-ended questions that invited youngsters not only to talk about the objects they were showing, but also to think about the nature of the objects.

But over time, show-and-tell can get stale for children and teachers. Children's attention often wanders, and acting out increases. Another problem is the mounting insecurity of children who feel that the toys or special possessions they bring don't measure up. This problem is particularly acute in January, when many youngsters have new toys to show off. It's important to be sensitive to all children's feelings; after all, group time is supposed to be about sharing, self-esteem, and expression, not competition.

Show-and-Teach

For these reasons, it may be time for a new and improved approach to show-and-tell: Show-and-Teach! The Show-and-Teach approach preserves family involvement and, at the same time, shifts the focus from material objects (which are too easily judged and compared) to projects, ideas, and skills. With Show-and-Teach, children have an opportunity to teach something they know to the class. It could be something they made, a song, a sound, or even a way to jump or snap fingers — whatever they think is special. One child brought in a sculpture she had created with newspaper and rubber bands and explained how she had made it.

There's another plus to giving show-and-tell a facelift: Children often love to become the teacher. With Show-and-Teach, they get the opportunity to take on that role as they teach something they know to everyone — including you!

Many young children love to have homework like the big kids. Why not give children an assignment to bring in something specific for Show-and-Teach? For example, invite them to show something that makes a noise, rolls, or opens and closes. Maybe something that is very tiny or a special color, shape, or size. Or ask children and their families to find or make something related to a specific place, event, or book. Don't forget to record the results on an experience chart or a graph!

Looking at Children's Development

 ou can tie every part of your curriculum into group time. In group meetings you can develop and enhance a multitude of social-emotional, cognitive, creative, and physical skills.

Social & Emotional Development

What Children Do

• Children naturally express their feelings by sharing personal news, resolving conflicts, dancing and singing, and discussing stories.

• Children communicate and cooperate with each other. When children listen to a book together, create a new verse for a song, or collectively solve a problem, they are simultaneously learning to share, take turns, and express ideas.

• Children's self-esteem flourishes when they experience themselves as accepted and contributing members of a group. Children learn they are capable of achieving success when they have opportunities to express their ideas through creative and cognitive expression.

Ways to Assist

• Provide literature that encourages children to discuss their feelings about a current topic or concern. (See *The Moral of the Story*.)

• Create a safe circle-time environment in which children know that it is okay to talk about their feelings without judgment or ridicule. (See *Talking About Feelings*.)

• Use games, songs, books, and discussions that invite children to consciously and creatively interact with each other. (See *Discovering Each Other*.) Set the stage for group conflict discussion and resolution. (See *Solving Problems, Creative Thinking Through Collaboration*.)

• Support children's individual expression of who they are and what they know through circle time activities that invite them to celebrate themselves, their ideas, and their families. (See *Talking About Feelings, Thinking About Families, Creating Curriculum Together*.)

Physical Development

What Children Do

• Children develop gross-motor skills in forms of creative and expressive movement through circle games and music and movement activities.

• Children explore their bodies as they move through space. They develop their coordination and spatial awareness as they move around and among one another.

• Children develop fine-motor skills when they participate in fingerplays, hand motions, drawing, and writing activities at group time.

• Children explore rhythm through a wide range of both fine- and gross-motor activities. When they dance or clap to rhythms and beats, children explore the different sound-motion combinations they can make and follow.

• Children develop physical control and the ability to relax their bodies through sitting in a group.

Ways to Assist

• Invite children to move freely without a directed structure. Allow them to independently explore different size, shape, direction, and tempo movements.

• Encourage children to test their skills in rhythmic dance and outdoor games. (See *Fun With Rhythm, Let's Go Outside, Feeling the Music, Say It With Puppets*!)

• Use rhythm instruments and rhythmic clapping patterns to orchestrate a favorite song or story. Add even more physical movement by creating a marching band! (See *Playing With Patterns*.)

• Help children relax and work out body kinks and fidgets through simple stretches and relaxing breathing.

Cognitive Development

What Children Do

• Expressive and receptive language skills are fostered. Most group time activities invite children to speak and listen; many encourage children to read books and charts and create and write their own verses or stories. Children also develop phonemic awareness by exploring words and sound together.

• The language and vocabulary of math are developed as children make comparisons of how much or how many, big or little, long or short, more or less. Solving problems as a group helps children stretch their own thinking and develop new strategies.

• Children use science-process skills of observation, prediction, experimentation, and evaluation in group activities that invite them to explore themselves and the world around them. Children might investigate an object from nature, a toy car, an animal, or even food.

Ways to Assist

• Create a print-rich environment filled with literature, Big Books, puppets, flannel board stories, word charts, songs, and poems that encourage children to use an abundance of language, reading, and writing skills. (See *Say It With Puppets!*) Ask thought-provoking questions that invite children to engage in wordplay and open-ended conversations. (See *Talking With Children, Playing With Words*.)

• Invite children to make comparisons and quantify their world by asking questions such as "How many children are at circle time? Are there more children with sneakers or shoes?" or "What is the smallest book on the shelf?" (See *Measuring, Graphing & Estimating, Make Math an Everyday Experience*.)

• Model scientific thinking and problem solving by being curious about the objects around the room. Questions such as "What would happen if …?" model the sense of wonder that is key to scientific inquiry. (See *Predicting Together, Exploring and Questioning, Discovering Through the Five Senses*.)

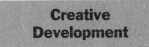

Creative Development

What Children Do

• Children use fluid, flexible, and creative-thinking skills by exploring ideas together, both real and fantasy.

• Children find new uses for objects as they apply creative and problem-solving skills.

• Children stretch their imaginations as they create groups stories

and sing songs about imaginary people and places and respond to open-ended questions.

• Children develop life-long aesthetic-appreciation skills by sharing perceptions with one another. Whether it is a beautiful flower, song, poem, dance, or piece of junk, notice children describe and appreciate what is beautiful in the world.

Ways to Assist

• Be open to children's creative suggestions. What may seem like a strange idea at first may be the germ of a terrific new concept or activity. Don't think you have all the answers — instead invite children to think of ways to solve problems for you! (See *Creative Thinking Through Collaboration, Imagine That!*)

• Introduce a new toy, a unique tool, an instrument, or a picture as an overture to creating new uses for objects. Questions such as "What can you do with…?" or "How many ways can you use…?" get children's thinking in motion. (See *Creating Curriculum Together, There's Music in Me*.)

• Celebrate the beauty in everything. Bring in something every day (a beautiful leaf, bean, book, rock, stick) for children to see, touch, and appreciate. Invite children to use different words to describe what they see and how the object makes them feel.

• Bring art materials to group time to give children an opportunity to brainstorm ideas and create something together.

• Ask questions that invite creative responses, such as, "If you were a monkey, what would your school look like?" Record children's responses.

Making
Collaborative Decisions

Even as adults, it is not always easy to make decisions as a group. Sometimes it is impossible to reach a consensus. In the classroom community, most of each child's time is spent in a group. Collaborative decision-making is therefore critical!

Using Group Time Effectively

Group decision-making involves carefully considering everyone's ideas, then working together toward and finally reaching consensus on how to solve a problem. It's an important process for young children to undertake, as it builds valuable social and cognitive skills.

Decision-Making

Implementing their ideas and decisions with your guidance fosters children's self-esteem as they watch their own plans unfold in their classroom.

Here are some ways to help children move through the decision-making process together:

Warm Up. Prepare your group for making decisions together by playing some simple cooperative games like "Blanket Toss" (children grasp the edge of a blanket and together toss a ball in its center) or "Clapping Names" (one clap for each syllable of a child's name). The spirit of cooperation and group unity that develops will carry over into the group's decision-making activities.

Discuss Decisions. Talk about what a decision is. Ask children about choices they've made today, such as what to wear. Allow time for several ideas to be introduced, and encourage the conversations that develop.

As children become more familiar with how choices are made, you can discuss simple parts of the curriculum for the group to make decisions about. You may start by assessing the job chart together, planning the next field trip, or choosing which story to act out for an end-of-year show.

Brainstorm and Record Ideas. Recording ideas from your group discussions through writing, mapping, and drawing is an important step in decision-making. Children should be free to express themselves through a variety of methods and materials as they brainstorm ideas.

Build Consensus. Reaching consensus among children can happen in many ways, depending on the needs of the group. You may ask them to simply look around and notice if everyone agrees. In other cases, it may be appropriate for the group to vote. To count the vote, children may tally by number or compare "more" and "less."

Follow Through. Once a consensus has been reached, guide children as they implement their group decision. The sooner this happens after the actual decision, the better.

You may be asking "Are all the children in my class really ready to make group decisions?" Naturally, you should be sensitive to the individual social and emotional needs of children in your group. Some may need direct help from you before they're able to use decision-making skills.

Group decision-making involves communication, timing, cooperation, imagination, respect, tolerance, patience, and leadership skills. Remember: Practicing the group decision-making process is just as important as the result.

Planning Tips

■ **Establish an identity.** Talk about every child. Find ways to document who makes up your group.

■ **Make it predictable.** Children respond better to regular routines and well-organized group systems.

■ **Brainstorm rules.** Let children help establish rules for group time and for cooperative games.

■ **Include everyone.** Ensure that every child's ideas are used in some way.

■ **Acknowledge children's rights.** Children have a fundamental right to be recognized and accepted by you and by one another. If you nourish these rights, your group will be cohesive and supportive.

■ **Model respect.** Your equal treatment of children and recognition of everyone's attempt to participate will create the best foundation for great group times throughout the year.

Getting
to
KNOW ONE
ANOTHER

As we help children learn about one another's likes and
dislikes, and about our cultures and families, we acknowledge
the richness and diversity of our classroom community and
foster important social/emotional skills.

Discovering Each Other

During your group times early in the year you may feel that you are meeting with a sea of individuals rather than a close-knit group — and you are! It takes time for children to learn how to interact together. But creating this sense of community — working on it together — builds not only individual feelings of self-worth but also a strong group identity that fosters learning and pride. Children may need time and assistance in developing an understanding of group needs as well as individual differences. You can facilitate this process by acknowledging what each child has to say and by modeling how to contribute ideas.

Welcoming Everyone

Try these guidelines to foster a spirit of community.

■ **Welcome every child warmly to circle time.** Make it clear to each one that you're glad he or she is there.

■ **Listen closely to children's ideas.** Your positive attitude and nonjudgmental responses help children to view their own ideas as valid.

■ **Be a role model for cooperation.** Your acceptance of others encourages children to be open to new points of view.

■ **Point out similarities and differences in children.** As you and your class discuss the ways people are different, bring out some ways children are alike.

■ **Encourage children to ask each other questions.** Invite child-to-child interactions by having children ask or answer questions for you.

Learning to Listen

In building group feeling, it's important to help children learn how to listen to one another. Like adults, children feel they are valued when they are listened to and when they feel the support of others. The younger children are, the more difficult it is for them to listen to one another. Keep the groups small and their sharing time limited.

Reflective listening is a technique often used by adults that you can also teach four- and five-year-olds. It involves helping children to listen to one another and then reflect on what the speaker said. Begin by saying "Let's see how good we are at listening. We'll all listen carefully to what Esther says. After she's through speaking, see if you can tell me what she said." When Esther is through, follow up with "Who can tell me something Esther said?" Ask a number of children to add what they heard.

There are two important results of this process: Children listen more closely, and the person sharing feels supported as she hears her thoughts expressed by someone else in the group. This is a particularly good technique to use during personal sharing time or even during show-and-tell.

Solving Problems

When problems arise, bring children together and ask them what they think needs to be done — not because you want them to arrive at a solution you've already decided on, but because their own suggestions will probably be the most effective in meaningfully resolving the dispute.

If a group is trying to work together but is still having problems, step back and just observe for a while. If no one is in any danger of being hurt, resist the temptation to jump in and settle their dilemma. You may have already found that children can work out problems themselves with time.

The Members of the Group

Remember, every group is a collection of individuals and you want to celebrate each one!

One way to focus on individuals at group time is to let each child have a celebration day that's all her own. For example, at group time, invite Tasha to tell about herself and the things she brought.

Then help children see how their individual contributions can help build a sense of classroom community. Developing a Group identity helps children find a place for themselves in the larger context of your school. Children will keenly observe you as you model consideration, cooperation, and understanding. After all, community is what an early childhood setting is really all about.

Talking About Feelings

Many children feel they are the only ones who experience certain feelings. And children, like adults, take comfort in finding out that they are not alone. One of the most difficult things for children to deal with in the beginning of the year is separation from their families. They need opportunities to express their strong feelings freely.

Separation Sensitivity

Some people fear that discussing separation feelings may open up a floodgate of despair, but group sharing of these important feelings as they happen eases their intensity. By fostering this kind of openness and encouraging freedom of expression, you are a true advocate for children's feelings.

At group time, you are creating a safe place for children to share with one another. And this kind of intimate conversation, similar to a family discussion, reassures children that their school is a place where they can express both negative and positive feelings, a place where they will be listened to.

At one time it was thought that adults should redirect children or even deny their feelings when they said they missed Mommy and Daddy. But this thinking denies very appropriate and important feelings, causing children to submerge their emotions beneath a facade.

The best way to deal with feelings is to bring them out and talk about them. Encourage other children to share what they are thinking, and share your own feelings.

Practical Planning

Group time is one of the best times to develop a sense of family and community among your children.

One important goal for your first group time sessions is to help children feel welcome and comfortable. Start slowly with very short, very informal large-group gatherings. If you are relaxed and conversational, your children will be too. Welcome each child individually, saying his or her name and making eye contact. Acknowledge everyone in some way. For instance, you might say, "What a wonderful smile you're wearing today, Jesse." Then briefly share how you are feeling, and ask others to tell how they feel.

After you've become familiar with individual family configurations, plan informal discussions that start with nonthreatening, open-ended questions, such as "I wonder what your families are doing today. What do they do while you are here?"

Talking about what Mom, Dad, or Grandpa is doing gives children a sense of perspective about their separation and helps them remember that even though the important adults in their lives are away and busy right now, they will be back later. And that gives them the peace of mind to focus on learning.

Keeping It Simple

It's important not to force anyone to talk or share feelings. Children (like most adults) get nervous when a leader goes around the circle and expects them to take a turn. It's perfectly fine for a child to listen for most, if not all, of the year.

Remember, your beginning circle time sessions need to be short, informal, warm, and welcoming. Sit at children's level and make eye contact. Keep it personal and supportive. The time you take to create a sense of family will lay the foundation for wonderful group times and a rich and rewarding year.

Books on Feelings

These books may stimulate lively discussions.

Best Friends by Miriam Cohen (Macmillan)

Do You Want to Be My Friend? by Eric Carle (Thomas Y. Crowell)

Going to Day Care by Fred Rogers (G. P. Putnam's Sons)

Jamaica Tag-Along by Juanita Havill (Scholastic)

Jesse's Day Care by Amy Valens (Houghton Mifflin)

Sometimes I Feel Like a Mouse by Jeanne Modesett (Scholastic)

Timothy Goes to School by Rosemary Wells (Dial Books)

The Toughest, Meanest Kid on the Block by Ben Shecter (G. P. Putnam's Sons)

Whose Mouse Are You? by Robert Kraus (Scholastic)

Will I Have a Friend? by Miriam Cohen (Macmillan)

Thinking About Families

S haring family news comes naturally to young children. However, with the diversity of families in our society, such discussions require sensitivity. More and more children are a part of extended families, stepfamilies, and single-parent homes. It is more important than ever to incorporate different family types into everyday discussions and activities. By recognizing both traditional and nontraditional family groupings, you help children feel comfortable and positive about their families. At the same time, children can develop an understanding and appreciation of families that are different from theirs.

Getting to Know Your Families

Group time is a wonderful place to begin. In your discussion, support children and their families by avoiding the traditional description of a family as a mother, father, and children. Instead, define families by the things they do together and the feelings they share. For example, "A family is a group of people who live together. Families help and take care of one another, play and work together, love one another." Take time to let children talk about the other things that families do together. Help children see that although family members may differ from family to family, the characteristics that hold families together are often the same.

Family Changes

Families change through events like birth, death, divorce, marriage, adoption, and imprisonment. It's important to help children see that these events happen to many different families. A child may feel frightened or isolated because he thinks that it is only his family or only he is experiencing a particular event. Your sensitivity to particular situations can also inspire comforting conversations.

Bring families into conversations naturally. Rather than planning a set time to explore a specific family unit or theme, talk about families as they come up in children's discussions. Pick up on children's cues as they share their thoughts and experiences.

Learning About Families

Encourage discussions and play. Besides making sure that your dramatic-play area has a variety of family props, inspire play that involves different kinds of families by cutting out a variety of simply shaped felt people and pets of all sizes. Place these next to a felt board where children can easily play with them, tell stories, and create situations.

Encourage families to read. Invite children to borrow books to take home. (See box.) They might also like to share their family reading experiences the next day at group time. Consider inviting parents, grandparents, older siblings, aunts, and uncles to visit your program and read a favorite book. Reading together will help families feel closer and feel a part of your program. (Some people may be comfortable reading to a large group, while others might prefer sitting in a cozy corner reading to just a few children.)

Books About Families

These books will inspire discussions.

A Chair for My Mother and **Something Special for Me** by Vera B. Williams (Greenwillow)

A Father Like That by Charlotte Zolotow (Harper & Row)

First Pink Light by Eloise Greenfield (Thomas Y. Crowell)

Friday Night Is Papa's Night by Ruth Sonneborn (Puffin)

Grandmama's Joy by Eloise Greenfield (Putnam)

Is That Your Sister? by Catherine Bunin (Pantheon)

Lots of Mommies by Jane Severance (Lollipop Power)

My Mother and I Are Growing Strong by Inez Maury (New Seeds Press)

Sorely Trying Day by Russell and Lillian Hoban (Harper & Row)

A Song About Families

The verses can change with the configurations of the children's families.

We All Have a Family

(tune: "The Farmer in the Dell")

We all have a family.

We all have a family.

The people who live with us

Are all in our family.

Our (sister/brother/mother/etc.) is in our family.

Our (sister/brother/mother/etc.) is in our family.

The people who live with us

Are all in our family.

More "Family" Activities!

Try these ideas for more family fun at group time.

Encourage intergenerational contact. Warm and loving relationships develop when younger and older generations get to know each other. Speak to the director of a local senior-citizen center or residence about "adopting" a grandparent for your class. Find someone who loves children, is enthusiastic, and whom your children will find interesting, and ask him or her to come and visit.

Create a celebrations chart. Together, brainstorm a list of different ways in which families celebrate. Write children's ideas on an experience chart titled "How We Celebrate." To stimulate thinking and discussion, ask questions such as "What do you do to get ready for this celebration at your house? What foods do you eat?"

Share a personal experience. Children are always fascinated by their teacher's own experiences. Choose a special event to talk about, such as a graduation or a relative coming to visit. This helps children understand that family celebrations don't happen just at holiday times. You might discuss how you and your family bustled about to cook special foods and invited people over for a party.

Introduce a special show-and-tell. Invite children to bring in an object from home that is special to their family and hide it in a bag. Then, at group time, give clues so everyone else can try to guess what it is. Not only does this trigger discussion about children's homes and customs, but it also involves the class in problem solving.

Integrate family foods. Invite a child or a family member to visit and share a favorite recipe connected with the family's heritage. Make sure, though, to ask about other foods the family likes to eat at home. For example, as you enjoy Michael's mother's recipe for guacamole and chips, ask him to talk about and name some of his other favorites. (He'll probably include spaghetti and ice cream!)

Remember that when discussing families with children as a group, the goal is to celebrate every child's family, no matter how big or small, familiar or unique. Through these experiences, children share an important piece of themselves and learn new ways to respect and appreciate their own families — and those of others.

Keeping
Group Time Alive

Even experienced teachers sometimes face difficulty in keeping group time discussions actively flowing. It is a delicate balance between providing enough structure and direction for children and providing the freedom children need to express themselves.

Keep Group Time Valuable

Simplify your agenda so that group time is a relaxed time. Allow time during the meeting for children to share important information and feelings and express their individuality. Listen carefully to the information children share. It can be a valuable resource as you do curriculum planning, giving you insight into what children need.

Be a Model

Pay attention to each child by making eye contact and acknowledging his participation. This provides a model for children that is far more effective than admonishing them to be quiet and listen. Sharing your own thinking aloud also helps children.

Look at Group Time as a Process

Remember that a strong sense of group develops when every child has the experience of belonging. It takes time! Try not to be overly eager for children to learn to function as a large group.

Balance the needs of the whole group while still being responsive to individuals, particularly at the beginning of the year. Select short activities that acknowledge and include each child, and help all children learn about one another. Here are some ideas for games and songs to help you get started:

Name Games. A name is something that all children have, yet it is unique and important to each individual throughout the early childhood years. Begin by simply making eye contact with each child and greeting him by name or inviting each child to say hello to the person next to him.

You might also try going around the circle, asking each child to say his name and to clap a motion or make a special movement that everyone else repeats.

Guessing Games. Another favorite is creating a guessing game about each child. Start with "I Spy," saying "I spy a child who has brown hair, a blue shirt, red sneakers, and whose name starts with B!" Give a variety of clues to help children guess. Then let children become the leaders and give their own clues.

For kindergartners, make a poster with clues to the identity of one child written or drawn on it. Hide his name below the clues with a construction-paper flap. Reveal the name after children have made their guesses.

Most children will thrive on games that point them out individually and make them the focus of attention. However, be sensitive to and respect a child who chooses to be passed by. Keep inviting him to join in, but don't push. He may need time as a spectator before being comfortable enough to become a participant.

Early on, you set the tone that will make meeting time either a struggle that you have to manage or a relaxed experience to which everyone contributes. Setting that tone may mean losing your inhibitions, letting go, and making sure you are enjoying yourself.

This article was written by Michelle Sutherland, a kindergarten teacher in Boston, MA.

Group Time Tips

Pre-Kindergarten

■ **Ask lots of open-ended questions** to stimulate language skills.

■ **Start with short group times** and gradually lengthen them.

■ **Remember to be silly sometimes.** Be prepared with fun songs and rhymes.

■ **Play games** that help build children's ability to take turns.

Kindergarten

■ **Add a calendar and check-in activity.** Personalize this by including events important to individual children.

■ **Extend the length of meeting time** when needed, but remember that many children will still have difficulty sitting for long periods of time.

■ **Give children more responsibility** for creating rules and systems for group management. Write down the rules together.

CREATIVITY
Around
THE CIRCLE

What happens when a circle of children brainstorm together?

A collective of creative thinkers is born!

Group time can become a place

to create by sharing imaginations and materials.

Creative Thinking
Through
Collaboration

Group time is a daily opportunity to create a little magic or be a little silly. After everyone has gathered around, the teacher begins: "The strangest thing happened to me on my way to school this morning. I carried this big bag of art materials here, then I couldn't remember what we were going to make with them! Can you help me?"

With that, the teacher carefully spills out the materials — colored paper, sticks, yarn, strips of cloth — and asks, "What do you think we could do with these things?"

Soon children are bursting with ideas: "kites," "masks," "houses." Everyone is filled with excitement.

Why Is Creative Thinking Important?

In this creative-thinking discussion, the teacher sets the stage and then makes space for children to take over the thinking process. As teachers, we all have to watch the amount of time we spend talking at children. After all, telling someone about things does not fully engage her creative thinking. But asking someone to think about something invites her to take ownership in the process and encourages higher-level thinking.

Creative thinking is a life skill, one that children can apply to everything they do for the rest of their lives. As you know, memorizing facts and figures is not what makes a child a thinker. Rather, it is the ability to use information creatively, flexibly, and with ingenuity that is important — that is intelligence. It is the ability to think, learn, and experiment with language and objects that helps children achieve these goals.

Creativity — Any Time, Any Place

Help make creative thinking a part of everything children do.

Give children problems to solve, questions to ponder, and challenges to try, and your group will be off and running. Try these kick-off ideas:

Start with a question. Bring in a collection of small, medium, and large cardboard boxes. Then ask children an open-ended question such as "How many different ways can we use boxes?" Give children time to discuss, experiment, and create together.

Start with a prop. Unique props encourage children to think and to share ideas. Any shyness they feel often disappears as they become involved and interested in a machine or ladybug puppet.

Start with a challenge. For example, you might offer children creative-movement challenges, and then invite them to make up some of their own. Put on some lively music, and play a modified follow-the-leader game. Start with a simple "Can you do this?" challenge such as clapping hands.

Next, invite children to take turns making challenges for everyone else to try. Ask questions such as "How can we move this Ping-Pong ball across the table without touching it?" After you pose a question, provide time to test it out.

Creating Creativity

■ **Pose open-ended questions,** some as simple as "How many different ways can you use a banana?"

■ **Give children time to think and listen** to each other as they brainstorm realistic and fanciful ideas.

■ **Start out with realistic suggestions,** such as making a banana split or baking a pie, and then move on to more imaginative ideas like using the banana as a play telephone or a pretend pencil.

■ **Offer concrete objects** like a key, leaf, stick, or sheet of paper, to stimulate thought

■ **Provide a variety of materials** like blocks and boards, magnifying glasses, and art materials. Children can use them to discover and solve problems together.

Great Group Creations

Try some of these ideas for some great collective creations!

■ **Mural Drawing** to music with crayon, chalk, or pastel

■ **Weaving Natural Materials** (dried grasses, weeds, feathers) through yarn strips strung across the branches of a dead tree bough. This looks great hanging from your ceiling.

■ **Collective Pass-Around Pictures.** Children draw to music, but when it stops they pass their picture to the child on the right, who continues drawing. The pictures continue around the circle until the drawings get back to the original children!

■ **Group Mobile** of scrap paper and other materials

■ **The Longest Cooperative Paper Chain** in the World!

Start with a starter. Create something for the group to finish in their own way. You might set up a few blocks in an unusual way, then invite children to discuss the "starter" building and talk about their visions of what they would like to do with it.

A Group Art Project

Circle time is a great place to rev up your group's creative-thinking engines and let them take off into the world of process art. They say that two heads are better than one, so just imagine what happens when you put ALL of your children together on art projects. Creativity blossoms as children share ideas and techniques. Social skills benefit from the opportunity to problem-solve together. Children learn the importance of listening and responding to each other, of taking turns and sharing.

Step 1: Collective Planning

One class decided to create a group sculpture out of recycled materials. The first day, children brainstormed ideas freely. They discussed the materials they wanted to use and where they might find them, recording their ideas on chart paper. They agreed to look at home for recycled materials they could add to the classroom storehouse. Through an active discussion, children decided what would and wouldn't work ... core curriculum for the development of critical-thinking skills!

Step 2: Collective Thinking

Several days later the group filled the center of their group time circle with the inspiring pile of recycled materials they had collected. Children's conversations were animated as they suggested ways to use this wonderful junk. The teacher's role was to stimulate ideas through open-ended questions ("What should we use for a base? How will we attach the materials?") and to organize materials. Once everyone had had a chance to express ideas, the group reached a consensus about what material they would like to use as a base. They were ready to start creating their group sculpture.

Step 3: Collective Construction

Children experimented with different ways to attach their beautiful junk onto the base. Some pieces wouldn't stay on or fit the way they expected, but with the teacher's help children learned it was okay to make mistakes and gained valuable insights from them. They understood the importance of trying different approaches and strategies.

As the group sculpture began to emerge, some children thought it looked like a dinosaur or dragon. The teacher continued to stimulate their ideas and creativity by asking, "If this were a dinosaur, where would its head be? What color would it be? Are there any materials here that look like a dinosaur's nose?"

Over several weeks, children read books about dinosaurs, talked about whether their dinosaur could fly and what it ate, and where it lived. They continued to bring in materials from home like a variety of shiny paper to make scales and even wrote a book about their friend. Finally, they named their dinosaur, and placed him in a place of honor in the room.

As you plan creative group-problem-solving experiences like this one, remember that you are providing your children with learning tools they will use over and over again throughout their schooling and their lives.

Creating Curriculum Together

Everyone's out on the playground enjoying the warm October day. Suddenly a few children call out "Come see what we just found!" Others run to see the new discovery — a giant anthill covered with ants scurrying about their work. A spontaneous group has formed and the teacher uses their interest to encourage observation and discussion.

She invites children to ask their own questions. "What do ants eat?" asks one child. Another wonders where ants live and whether ants are friends with other insects.

Questions That Shape Curriculum

Back in the room, the teacher invited the children to discuss their experience. She asked open-ended questions, such as "What surprised you? What did you learn that you didn't know? What would you like to find out about ants? How might we do that?" She generated a list of the children's ideas, which included reading books about ants, creating a classroom ant farm so they could watch how ants live over a period of time, and inviting classroom visitors who knew about ants (like the school janitor) to visit and share their knowledge. After several weeks of studying ants during group and activity time, children created a group book about ants, which they illustrated and placed in the language center.

This group time exploration was especially successful because the inspiration came directly from children and, therefore, built on their own natural curiosity. The teacher hadn't planned on having group time in the playground, nor had she intended to focus on ants this fall. Yet, nature provided the topic and the children have contributed their excitement. Without preplanning or expensive materials, the teacher knew how to make the most of a spontaneous event.

A spontaneous group time can become as involved as you and your children want it to be. Focus on reading children's interest and being ready to learn more together, or tune in to whether just watching and discussing will be enough. Remember, every spontaneous group time does not need to unfold into a "lesson" or extend into a formal activity; it can have great simplicity and child-centeredness.

Curriculum Created by Children

Children often have their own theories about the world in which they live. By discussing them, we get a picture of how they are thinking. In the scenario above, some children's thoughts sprang from what they'd seen. Other children were synthesizing ideas, applying a past experience to the current event. For example, they may have previously noticed ants carrying away a cookie crumb from their picnic blanket. This observation may have led them to believe that ants eat chocolate chip cookies.

From this rich soil of interest and curiosity, a theme emerged. The same steps can be used to create

---

Developing Themes

Try these ideas for child-created curriculum:

■ **Select a theme together.** It can come from an event, an interest children have demonstrated in the class, or from a brainstorming session at group about topics to study.

■ **Check prior knowledge.** Ask children to share what they already know about the topic.

■ **Generate questions to investigate.** Ask children what else they would like to find out.

■ **Brainstorm activity ideas.** Invite children to suggest activities and methods for finding out more.

■ **Generate a schedule.** Use a group calendar for loosely mapping out the children's activity ideas over time.

■ **Record the result.** When the theme work is finished, record what children have discovered.

Spontaneous Group Times

■ **Allow children to be in charge.** Rather than being quick to guide the experience, allow them to create a role for you to play.

■ **Be spontaneous!** People tend to be more creative when they are surrounded with spontaneous role models.

■ **Don't set specific parameters.** Spontaneous group times can vary in size, setting, and length, and either you or your children can be the initiators.

■ **Be flexible.** It's not unusual for a spontaneous group time to occur in the middle of a planned one.

■ **Be open to different settings.** Spontaneous group time can happen anywhere children are engaged in their normal play activities!

curriculum based on the simplest of ideas or everyday events.

Child-designed curriculum is cooperative learning at its best. It allows children to experience the joy of working collectively to create a common goal or to investigate a group question. It starts from where children are — their interests and prior knowledge — and builds to what they want to find out. Children often understand much more than teachers suspect. By hearing all their ideas, you can avoid making wrong assumptions in planning the activities, materials, and topics to explore.

Enjoying the Benefits

Wonderful things happen when children invent curriculum together as a group. They become active participants in their own learning and gain a stronger sense of self-esteem. They also discover from one another that there are many ways to answer questions and to find out more. They realize that, with only a little guidance from you, they can do it on their own!

Although there are many different ways spontaneous group times can originate with the children, don't forget that you can foster these times too. When you see something interesting or when an important event happens in your life, it's your turn to be the initiator. By doing this you also provide a wonderful model for spontaneous events. The secret? Be prepared to drop whatever you are doing to make the most of a spontaneous group time — whenever and wherever you are. It's worth it!

Rainbow Ideas

What makes the colors in the rainbow?
Joey: Nature paints them.
Angela: Sunshine does it.

Imagine That!

Fantasy and reality, during early childhood years, are separated by a fine line. Children often cross this line to create worlds where they are in charge of all kinds of amazing feats. During these magical journeys, children explore their own creativity.

As the teacher, you are an integral part of this process. By providing encouragement in the form of props, ideas, and problems to solve, you can stimulate incredible sessions of make-believe. Remember that there are no right or wrong ways to participate.

The following activities offer beginning suggestions for using guided imagery and fantasy at circle time.

No More Monsters!

As the teacher, you can help dispel scary myths and provide children with many opportunities to discuss fantasy and reality. Try these techniques:

■ **Is It Real? Is It Pretend?** Collect a variety of pictures for categorizing as real or pretend. Encourage children to discuss what makes a real or pretend character or event.

■ **Things That Scare Me.** Tell children something that frightens you. Then make an experience chart of the things that scare your children. Together, talk about whether these things need to be scary.

■ **Things That Go Bump in the Night.** Encourage children to draw a nightmare. It might be a picture of how it looks or how it feels.

■ **Make Monster Shadows.** Use a flashlight in back of a large sheet to make a "shadow screen." Have children take turns going behind the screen to make monster shadows.

Share a Musical Voyage

Take children on a musical voyage to a mystery world. Use a classical musical piece such as *"The Sorcerer's Apprentice"* by Paul A. Dukas to set the mood. Have children sit cross-legged in a circle. Explain that you are all going to take a voyage without even leaving the room. Tell children that as the music plays you will describe places and scenes. They won't need to talk out loud, only imagine pictures and feelings in their minds.

Begin by saying "Today we are going to take a wonderful journey on a giant magic carpet that will hold our entire class. Now, buckle your seat belts." Encourage children to listen to the music, then ask, "What do you see as we travel through the sky?" Through your questions and comments, help children feel that they are on their way to a magic castle where a great magician makes his potions.

Remember to end the journey by safely returning the carpet to the classroom. Your tone of voice and sense of wonder and involvement will contribute greatly to the success of this activity. You can alter this activity according to children's moods and interests. They might pretend to float on a canoe down a river that travels through a magical forest, or be a butterfly flying high above the world.

Act Out a Wonderful Story

The best creative dramatic situations are those that are spontaneous and grow from a popular idea. For example, suggest that children use their imaginations to take a trip to the moon. Then ask, "What clothes will we need for our journey to the moon?" Together, pretend to put on a space suit, heavy boots, and a helmet. Do this slowly so children really feel how heavy the space clothing is. Invite everyone to get in the pretend spaceship and buckle up. Prepare for the blastoff together and begin your journey. Ask children to tell you what they see outside their windows.

Upon landing, put on soft, "floaty" music and move lightly together. Use balloons as pretend moon rocks, and play a game of catch. End with a return to the spaceship and blast off for home.

Can You Be ... ?

Try quiet pretending with your class. Pose questions for children to act out, such as "Can you be a snowball melting in the sun? A cloud floating above a rainbow? A duck floating gently on a lake? A sleepy bird who has landed on a tree limb and is folding up its wings for a night's rest?" Try using one of these before storytime to set the mood for quiet listening. Children can suggest others to act out.

LITERACY & GROUP TIME

*Within the circle of children, communication
ignites children's desire to express themselves in speech,
drawing, and writing — while books and
stories become the vehicles to take them to faraway lands.*

Classroom Communication

Communication is one of the key elements that support pre-reading, and later, reading skills. And talking is one of the most important language activities in which children can participate. Studies have shown that having a variety of activities contributes to a good language and pre-reading program. Many of these activities can be done at group time. Such activities include listening to literature and poetry, dictating words and stories, making and maintaining classroom calendars, playing listening games, and participating in songs and fingerplays.

Call-and-Response

Feed My Cow

Teacher: Did you feed my cow?
Children: Yes, Ma'am!
Teacher: Will you tell me how?
Children: Yes, Ma'am!
Teacher: Oh, what did you give her?
Children: Corn an' hay.
Teacher: Oh, what did you give her?
Children: Corn an' hay.

Teacher: Did you milk her good?
Children: Yes, Ma'am!
Teacher: Did you do like you should?
Children: Yes, Ma'am!
Teacher: Oh, how did you milk her?
Children: Swish! Swish! Swish!
Teacher: Oh, how did you milk her?
Children: Swish! Swish! Swish!

Sharing the News

Encourage children to share events that have happened at home or school. The news might be about a class trip or Sarah's new family pet. Write down the news on an experience chart that children can illustrate.

From time to time, put together a classroom newspaper. Write or type (with a primary typewriter) your children's news reports. Leave blank areas above the stories so that children can later illustrate them. Duplicate these and send home a copy of the newspaper to share with parents. This is a wonderful way to keep parents informed about what's happening at school.

Select classroom news reporters to make important announcements at group time. Reporters can be rotated regularly and can wear a special tag to identify them. They can announce the date, special activities, birthdays, and the snack for the day.

In most classrooms, discussion of the weather is popular at group time, and it helps develop communication skills and comparative language. Each day select a weather reporter to look out the window, tell the class what he or she sees, and then attach a symbol or picture to the calendar representing the weather for the day.

For Younger Children

Here are a few group time suggestions related to language and listening for younger children.

Looking at Pictures. An interesting picture or poster can catch children's attention, even if it's just for a short time. Encourage them to name what they see, to use words to describe it, and to make the connection between a real object and a representation of one. Help children make these comparisons by matching concrete objects to pictures.

Listening Activities. Perhaps one of the most difficult tasks for younger children is to listen. Yet this is an important area for them to develop. Play listening games such as "No-Losers Simon Says," or use chants, such as the one in the box, in which children listen and imitate sounds or actions given by the leader. Other possible activities include having children guess familiar sounds of hidden animals or objects. Use pictures or objects, and encourage children to imitate the sounds they make. Then have them match similar objects with similar sounds.

Creative Calendar Tips

Try these ideas to make your calendar more meaningful.

■ **Give children an opportunity to mark special events** in their personal and family lives, such as birthdays, special trips, and the arrival of new siblings.

■ **Include special events** in the life of the classroom, such as the arrival of a new pet, an important holiday or vacation, or a show for parents.

■ **As the year progresses,** invite older children to help you make the calendar each month, including drawing the lines with a ruler or straightedge and writing the words and numbers.

Creating Calendars

It may be useful for older preschoolers and kindergartners, who are starting to develop a sense of time and sequence, to know the days of the week and to sometimes practice the order of numbers. However, repeating this activity day after day can become tedious for you and the children. Think about your calendar not only as a way to mark time, but also as a way to collectively record the daily experiences, events, ideas, and observations that are important and meaningful to your children. Also, actually creating calendars with children can support their self-expression, as well as foster self-esteem and problem solving. Here are some ideas to help you use this standard group time ritual for creativity and sharing.

Calendar Journal.

This is a simple way to create a beautiful calendar that really belongs to children, without spending hours cutting out numbers and shapes. Start by drawing a calendar grid of three- to four-inch squares on a large, heavy sheet of chart paper. Leave the squares of your calendar blank except for the dates written in small numbers in the corners.

Each day at calendar time, choose one child to fill in the next square on your calendar. Ask him what is important to him or what he would like to do that day and how he would like to fill in his square on the calendar. You might ask, "How are you feeling today?" or "What did you do or see before school?" or "What's special about today?"

Thumbs-Up, Thumbs-Down Days. Ask children each day whether it's a thumbs-up day or a thumbs-down day, and why. Give them an opportunity to discuss and debate what is good or bad about the day, and then take a vote. You can record the vote with arrows or have children trace their thumbs pointing up or down in that day's calendar square.

Is Today a Lion or a Lamb? Tracking the weather can help children become more aware of their surroundings and build their observation skills. Sun, cloud, and rain drawings work well early on; however, look for ways to vary children's observations and record-keeping each month. For example, you can keep track of the number of days it doesn't rain in April or the changes that are visible in May.

Talking With Children

Children are acutely sensitive to how their thoughts, opinions, and feelings are being accepted. The welcoming, positive message you send out through your body language, tone of voice, and choice of words tells children that their thoughts and feelings are respected and valued.

Take a few moments to think about how you talk to and listen to children. Are you an attentive listener? Do you ever half-listen while doing something else? Take note of your own listening and speaking skills. As children feel comfortable, the thoughts and feelings they share with you and with each other will add joy and pleasure to everyone's experience.

Taking Turns

It isn't always easy to take turns, but children will find it less difficult if they understand the system to follow.

■ **Discuss the importance of not interrupting** others before group discussions begin.

■ **Plan to devote time** to letting children freely respond to one another and to allowing one child to have the floor for as long as she needs it.

■ **Try sitting in a group** and rolling a ball to the person who is speaking. Children will learn that the person holding the ball has the floor. When another child speaks, the first child can roll the ball to him.

■ **Use a Native American "talking stone."** Only the person holding the stone can talk. Your children might enjoy finding their own special stone or other object and sharing it during group time.

Open-Ended Discussions

Open-ended discussions are the heart of group time. Because there are no right or wrong comments, there are also no wrong answers, and children quickly learn that everyone's ideas count. This enables them to experiment with ideas without the fear of being wrong. When children feel encouraged to talk and take risks with their ideas, they begin to use higher-level thinking skills such as application, analysis, and synthesis as they think creatively.

Communicating With Children

Children feel valued and are more apt to listen attentively when you make eye contact. And use friendly, inviting postures and gestures to invite children to continue.

Allow children to speak without interruption. You might consider splitting the group between two adults so there is more time for talking and listening. Help other adults model listening behavior, and talk with other teachers, assistants, and aides in your room about why it's important to be attentive. Invite them to join in at group time, sharing in children's delightful conversations.

Don't be afraid of silence. Everyone needs thinking time. Children are still learning and growing.

Keep the Conversation Going ...

The secret of a good open-ended discussion lies in the kind of questions you ask. Divergent questions such as "Would you tell me more?" and "What else do you think might happen?" encourage children to problem-solve and express themselves creatively.

Convergent questions such as "What is this?" and "Is this red?" have right and wrong answers and tend to limit discussion. Because they can be answered in just a word or two, there is little problem solving required.

Making Talking Fun

A new object can ignite a wonderful conversation and allow adults to facilitate instead of lead a discussion. You might bring in a delicate seashell, a friendly live animal, tinkling wind chimes, or a touchable musical instrument. When you present the object, you might ask questions such as "What could you do with this?" "What does it remind you of?" or "Where do you think it came from?"

Sit back together and enjoy stories that children relate about their lives and experiences. Encourage them to elaborate and bring other children into the conversation by asking divergent questions that will involve everyone. Have fun turning real-life experiences into fantasy expeditions and wonderful journeys of the imagination!

Say It With Puppets!

It's group time. As usual, the children gather, some eager to participate, others more reticent. But within minutes there's an entirely different atmosphere. Conversation is lively and animated. Children who rarely talk can't wait to share their experiences and ideas. What has worked this magic? A puppet named Gabby, who started the excitement simply by saying "Hi, Juanita. Look at your great smile! Tell me, what's making you smile?"

Puppets With a Purpose

Puppets can be the key to unlocking the voices of all your children, inviting them to be part of a special exchange. Most children don't even look at the puppeteer's face: They're watching the puppet's every move and tuning in to every word. Over and over again, we see that children will communicate to the puppet things they would never say to an adult or even to other children.

When using puppets, the important question to ask yourself beforehand is "What do I want to foster by using this puppet?" Is your goal to encourage children to participate? To talk about a specific issue? A problem? The following tips will help you and your puppet work magic in your classroom:

How to Use Puppets

Begin group time with a puppet. Let your puppet lead a hello song, talk about the weather, or share an experience. Children like seeing the puppet every day, and this routine will help them make transitions from and into other activities.

Introduce new concepts or themes with your puppet. Dress up your puppet for special occasions. "Welcome to red day!" Gabby greets children, decked out in her bright-red paper hat and cape. "Can you find something in our room that is red?"

Use puppets to involve children in activities. Many children's books include a puppet that represents the main character, which you can use to introduce the story. After you've read the story, invite children to ask the puppet questions or have the puppet ask them questions. "Can you help me write a new adventure?" the puppet might ask.

Invite children to use puppets. Let one start the puppet fun by asking questions, remarking on the day, or even posing a simple riddle. Once children have begun interacting with each other's puppets, sit back and watch their puppet talk develop.

Puppet Pitfalls

In working with puppets, keep the following pitfalls in mind:

Choose friendly looking puppets. Many children are afraid of puppets at first, so be sure to pick those that are more realistic than fantastic. Try people and small animals that have a warm, friendly appearance.

Remember: Size matters. Some large puppets fascinate adults but may be difficult for young children to manipulate. Start with small puppets that children can touch and feel comfortable with right away.

Break the ice. When first left alone with a puppet, children may have trouble knowing what to say or do. They may resort to aggressiveness. So be sure to model how to use puppets, and ask children to help them sing a favorite chant or song. They'll be fast friends before you know it!

Using Puppets

Used with care and thought, puppets can help you reach your children, even if they are troubled. The following tips can help.

■ **Make your puppet a confidant.** Your puppet can become a special friend to a child. "Do you ever get lonely like I do?" asks Gabby.

■ **Use puppets to help children resolve problems.** Your puppet can address situations in the classroom. Your puppet might say, "I feel like no one wants me to be their friend. How do you make friends?"

■ **Set aside "peace puppets"** to work out conflicts. When an argument arises, give children puppets (used only for this role), and help them talk about their feelings through the puppets.

■ **Ask puppets questions.** Shy children might be better able to express their thoughts and feelings if they pretend it is the puppet who's talking.

Playing With Words

One of the joys of group time is the opportunity for language play. Word play can highlight every aspect of language development. Younger children can practice listening, speaking, rhyming, and building vocabulary. Older children can work on identifying sounds and letters, as well as beginning reading and writing — all in a relaxed group setting in which children learn not only from you but from one another.

The social nature of language lends itself to the group experience. During group time, language is a means of communicating an idea or feeling, telling a joke or story, and making up a silly rhyme.

Building Word Play

Want to add more language games to your collection? These books offer many new ideas:

Creative Activities for Young Children by Mimi Brodsky Chenfeld (Harcourt Brace)

Language Games by Jean Warren (Monday Morning Books)

Wordsaroni: Word Play for You and Your Preschooler by Linda Allison and Martha Weston (Little, Brown)

Chicka Chicka Boom Boom by Bill Martin, Jr. and John Archambault (Gryphon House)

It Begins With A by Stephanie Calmenson (Gryphon House)

Silly Sally by Audrey Wood (Gryphon House)

Let's Do a Poem by Nancy Lauvick (Delacourt Press)

Richard Scarry's Just Right Word Book by Richard Scarry (Random House)

Playing Language Games

Lots of games can fill your linguistic playground. The following are a few suggestions to mix in with your old favorites:

Building With the Sounds of Words. Children love to play with the sounds of words. Real words like *lollipop* and *Mississippi* are not only fun to say but are also fascinating to see written down! And, of course, made-up words like *supercalifragilisticexpialidocious* are even more fun.

Invite children to keep a record of some of their favorite words on cards at group time to create a "wall of words." Encourage them to look and listen for new words to add throughout the year.

Playing With Letter Sounds. Older children are getting interested in letter sounds. They may notice that other children's names start with the same sounds as theirs: Bodhi, Belle, Bob, Beth. Play a letter-sounds game by chanting children's names that begin with the same sound. Invite those children to clap and add movements to go with their names.

Reciting Alliterative Poetry. This is another fun way to practice letter sounds. In the following call-and-response poem, the leader says a line and the children respond with the alliterative line. By repeating the response line, children hear the letter sound as they play with it. Try this poem:

Racing Red Raccoons
Riding up the hill, right there!
Racing red raccoons! (children)
Rounding to the corner, where?
Racing red raccoons! (children)
They go left, they go right!
Racing red raccoons! (children)
Now everyone is out of sight!
Racing red raccoons (children)

Rhyming Riddles. Children will enjoy the old game of "I'm thinking of something …" using riddles such as these:

I'm thinking of something on my face that sounds like the word *hose.* I'm thinking of something on your head that sounds like the word *deer.* I'm thinking of something on your leg that sounds like the word *me.*

Simon Says, "Listen." In this variation, children have to listen carefully and do what the leader says, not follow what she is doing. For example, you might say, "Touch your head" while you are actually touching your hips. This takes a lot of concentration and practice, so don't consider children "out" if they make a mistake.

Getting Forgetful. Another enjoyable language game is "Forgetful." You "forget" the words for things or use the wrong word in a sentence and encourage children to help or correct you. They'll be happy to oblige — and will be practicing their language skills too.

Making the Most of
Reading Aloud

There's a gentle feeling of excitement in the air. Everyone is looking for a good seat. Some children move so close they're almost on top of their teacher. What's going on? Storytime, of course!

Before You Begin

Once you've chosen a book to read aloud, consider the following:

Preview the book. Your group experience will be much richer if you have read the book at least once beforehand.

Prepare a comfortable and roomy read-aloud area. It's important that your storytime area be large enough that everyone can sit and see comfortably.

Introduce the book. You might look at the cover together and ask children to guess what they think the book will be about. This engages and involves them as readers. Mention the author and illustrator to reinforce the concept that people write and illustrate books.

Notice how you hold the book. Children need to be able to see the pictures. Therefore, it's important to hold the book wide open and to your side.

Give it all you've got. Dramatic and fun sound effects, hand motions, facial expressions, and changes in tone invite children to become part of the story with you.

Involve your listeners. If you are reading a repetitive story, give children a line to repeat, a hand motion, or a sound effect they can add at an appropriate time.

Develop ways to respond to questions. Children love to ask questions while you are reading, and you'll need to decide which ones to respond to. Some questions are important and need to be answered right away so the child will understand the rest of the story. Other questions will be answered in the story itself.

Take time for discussion. Children love to talk about a book you've just read. Take time afterward to encourage their questions and also to ask some of your own.

Choosing Books for Children

Check illustrations. Look for books that are clearly illustrated with colorful pictures. Since children will be "reading" the pictures while you are reading the words, it is important to have illustrations they can see well and that relate directly to what you are reading.

Look for a small amount of print per page. A good rule of thumb: If more space on the page is taken up by the words than by the picture, it is a book better read to children older than preschool age.

Find books that are predictable. Look for books that have repetitive language, rhythm, or rhymes that children can join in.

Use a variety of books. Provide opportunities for children to meet, through books, characters who have experiences similar to their own, as well as fantasy characters. Take your cues from the topics in which children express interest.

Reading aloud is one of the great joys of working with young children. Not only is it important for developing children's literacy skills, but it is also a time of great warmth and community. Reading together helps build children's social and emotional skills, as they bond with you and with their favorite characters!

A Magic Carpet

Let children know that storytime is a very special part of group time by rolling out a magic carpet.

- **Make a magic carpet** by drawing squares on a light-colored quilt or bedspread.
- **Ask children** to decorate it.
- **Once the magic carpet is complete,** make a big show of spreading it out at storytime. Ask children to think about where it might take them.
- **Invite children to climb on** the carpet for a ride.
- **Help children each find a spot** where they can see easily.
- **Remind them to stay on the carpet** so they don't "fall off" during the ride.
- **Put on some exciting music** to fly by. A good choice is the music from *Peter Pan*.
- **Then take off** for storyland.

Stories & Group Time:
Perfect Partners!

Something wonderful is happening. It's story time and today, instead of reading your group a book, you decided to tell them a story. Their intense looks tell you that they are living the tale. As the story unfolds, they have forgotten what is going on around them and entered a new place — an imaginary world that each of them has created in his or her own special way.

Storytelling is an art that is easily nurtured. We all tell stories every day — jokes, family events, complaints about what happened at the car repair shop are all forms of telling stories. Telling a story can be just as natural and even more rewarding if you take into consideration a few important steps.

Good Stories

Almost any story you enjoy sharing with children can make a good story to tell. It seems no one can ever have enough stories. The following books are collections filled with stories to tell.

The Complete Works of Hans Christian Andersen by Hans Christian Andersen (Avenel)

The Full Color Fairytale Book by R. C. Scriven (Crescent Books)

Paper Stories by Jean Stangle (Fearon Teacher Aids)

Pom-Pom Stories by Marj Hart and Walt Shelly (Fearon Teacher Aids)

How to Tell a Story

Get dramatic! Choose stories that have many dramatic elements. Children like to "see" and feel the events that are happening in stories. They can do this more easily when the plot features elements of suspense and surprise. Your expressiveness will lead the way.

Read or tell the story to yourself several times until it becomes a part of you. Each time you read the book, the characters and the sequence of events will flow more naturally. Having pictured the characters and events several times, you will be able to describe them more fully.

Use your own words. Using cards to help you remember the story will only interrupt the flow. Children want to hear the story in the way you tell it, so don't hesitate to recreate it in your own way, adding flourishes and details that you know will appeal to them.

Practice. Take the time to stand in front of a mirror and practice telling the story. A few run-throughs will give you the comfort level you'll need.

Move! Use your body and face to punctuate words, imitate events, and mirror emotions. Use silent pauses between events to engage children and add to the intrigue.

Involve children. Construct opportunities that invite children to recite repeating lines or phrases. Many children will do this spontaneously. By inviting them to join in, you welcome them into the world you are creating.

Tell emotional stories. Select some that will appeal to children's deepest feelings. Stories that mirror children's emotional experiences engage their minds and hearts and enable you to connect with children on a deeper level.

Relax and have fun. If you're having fun, children will too. Children will love the stories you tell.

It's Their Turn Now

Have you ever noticed that one thing you're talking about can remind a child of something else? This sparks a train of thought that becomes a long narrative having little to do with where you started. Many things children see or hear make them think of another idea they want to relate. Instead of struggling to keep them on track, why not make the most of their expressive energy by developing a co-operative circle story together?

Using Circle Stories

Here's how you can extend the learning value of each circle story:

■ **Use a tape recorder.** Place it inside the circle to record the story as children tell it. Then put the tape and the sack in the listening center, and encourage children to recreate the story.

■ **Transcribe the story** onto sheets of white drawing paper, leaving room at the top for children's illustrations. Reread or retell the tale at storytime.

■ **Give children a bigger role.** Invite each child to bring in one secret object from home to place in the sack.

Circle stories are easy to create. All you need is a colorful sack, such as a decorated pillowcase, and some interesting items to put inside. When collecting these objects, think of them as the elements of a story. Make sure you have at least as many items as you have children in your group. A mixture of stuffed animals or dolls and objects like toy vehicles, tools, plastic foods, and nature items can become the springboard to an exciting story line.

Don't be afraid to throw in something really unusual or even baffling. A group of four-year-olds created an amazing story when one child pulled a funnel from the sack!

Curtains Up

Once you've prepared the story sack, the fun begins. With the children seated in a circle, introduce the closed sack in a dramatic and mysterious way. Pique children's curiosity by passing it around for them to feel. Ask, "What could be in here? What will our story be about today?"

The first time you do this activity, you might model the storytelling process. Without looking, reach inside the sack, take out one object, and use it to begin the story.

(It's helpful to choose an animal or doll that can function as a main character.) Start with "Once upon a time," "Long ago and far away," or any other fun and intriguing opener, then kick off the story with the first thing that comes to your mind. If you pulled out a doll, you might say, "Sally was lonely, so she went to her friend's house."

Next, pass the sack to the child sitting beside you. Now it's his or her turn to reach inside, grab an object, and use it to continue telling the story of Sally. The sack — and the tale — continue around the circle, with each child taking a turn. Excitement builds as the story grows longer and the sack gets emptier. When the sack makes its way back to you, create a wonderful ending.

The Moral of the Story

You're reading a book or telling a fairy tale when cries of outrage burst from the group: "That's not fair! Why are they being so mean?" Whether the tale is real or imagined, your children have strong opinions about the characters' moral actions and are eager to share their beliefs.

Discussions about ethics can help children develop self-esteem, learn to resolve conflicts, and explore the meaning of right and wrong. Yet many teachers have found that these abstract subjects are difficult to discuss with young children, who learn best through concrete experiences. That's where storybooks come in.

Storybooks

The following books, which include many Cinderella stories, are bound to get everybody deliberating.

Aesop's Fables by Lisbeth Zwerger
(Picture Book Studio)

Ashpet: An Appalachian Tale
retold by Joanne Compton (Holiday House)

Cinderella by Marcia Brown (Scribners & Sons)

Fables by Arnold Lobel (Harper Junior Books)

Lon Po Po by Ed Young (Philomel)

Sootface by Robert San Souci (Dell)

The Egyptian Cinderella,

The Korean Cinderella, and

The Irish Cinderlad
by Shirley Climo (Thomas Y. Crowell)

The Rough-Faced Girl
by Rafe Martin (Putnam)

Turkey Girl by Betty Baker (Macmillan)

Cinderella's Many Faces

As children lose themselves in a story, they feel the characters' joys and sorrows. From there you can easily draw them into thoughtful conversations about personal values.

You'll soon discover that the deepest conversations and most worthwhile projects arise from children's spontaneous questions and answers. For example, after listening to the story of Cinderella, one kindergartner wondered out loud, "Why did Cinderella's stepsisters make her work so hard?" Instead of replying, the teacher asked the children for their opinions, then asked more questions. This led to a conversation in which children expressed their opinions about oppression and injustice and described how they felt when someone had treated them unfairly.

As a result of the discussion, children researched the Cinderella story and discovered that hundreds of Cinderella stories exist around the world. While the scenes and characters were slightly different, the theme remained the same. They discovered that people in different cultures share common human experiences and similar reactions to injustice.

Stories as Springboards

Fairy tales, fables, and proverbs feature good and evil characters, highlight ethical dilemmas, and address universal human issues and emotions, such as jealousy, prejudice, and hypocrisy. Here are some ways you can use stories to engage children in discussions:

Listen carefully. When you truly listen to children's questions — and answers — you open the door to understanding their thinking and beliefs. Ask yourself, "What are the children saying to me? What are their concerns? How can I best encourage this conversation?"

Ask more, answer less. Let children problem-solve. Don't provide answers. Instead, ask, "What do you think?" "Why don't you ask someone else in the class?" or "How can we solve the character's problem together?" This turns the discussion into a learning process.

Don't rush to judgment. Young children need to try different perspectives. They may side with the villain one day and with the hero the next. Remember that for young children the process of thinking about values is as important as determining the right answers.

There are many ways you can use literature to encourage conversations about values. Whatever strategy you use, remember that it's important for children to discover values based on their own experiences and thinking. Your children will especially remember and apply ethics when they take part in arriving at the conclusions themselves.

MATH & GROUP TIME

Math is more than numbers.

It is a language we use to express comparative, critical,

and logical thinking —

another way to see ourselves in relation to others.

Make Math an
Everyday
Experience

ath is all around us. Much of what we think, activities we're involved in, and even the comparative words we use involve beginning math concepts. We make comparisons as we do things, and the patterns we see tell us there is an order or sequence to life. Group time is a fertile ground for planting the seeds of good mathematical thinking and speaking.

The Language of Math

Math is more than basic concepts; it is also a language. Comparative words, such as *less than, more than, bigger,* and *smaller* are based on math concepts. Children can learn these words by using them in context — in relation to situations in your environment.

Incorporate the concepts of "more than" and "less than" by taking time to talk about the number of cloudy, rainy, or sunny days you've had during the week. Have there been more sunny days than cloudy? What kind of weather have you had the most? Or, together, sort crayons to see which color there is more of. Fill a jar with different-colored marbles, and invite children to estimate which color there is the most of. Then sort the marbles into piles, and line them up so everyone can see which color makes the longest line.

Concepts in Action

Learning to sort and classify is an important part of a child's mathematical growth. Bring in a bag filled with various objects — two of each kind. Ask children to sort the objects into pairs. You can also sort other items in your setting. For instance, you might gather all your

More Math Fun

■ **One-to-One Correspondence.** At group time, try movement activities in which each child has to match himself, one to one, with a partner.

■ **Patterning.** Keep patterns visual and auditory. For example, if you do a clapping pattern, show a drawing so children can see what the pattern looks like. Look at the visual pattern on the floor, ceiling, or around the room.

■ **Nonstandard Measurement.** Ask children to use nonstandard items to measure different things in your setting. For example, ask children to estimate how many crayons long the rug is and then do the actual measurement.

■ **Estimations and Predictions.** Use interesting items such as windup toys. Ask your group to predict which toy will go the farthest or be active the longest.

Math at Transition Time

Math activities are great ways to help children move from one activity to another.

■ **Counting Off.** Children count off in twos. All the ones hold up one finger and the twos hold up two. Then each child is excused by number group.

■ **The Magic Number.** Ask one child to say a magic number. Then touch each child as she counts off. When you reach that number, those children line up. Repeat until all children are in line.

■ **Foot by Foot.** Ask children to estimate the distance to the door. Then ask them to use their own feet to measure.

dress-up clothes and sort them in different ways.

When doing these activities, remember that it is important to sort the items in more than one way. If you are sorting beads, for instance, you might want to classify them once according to shape and another time according to color. Don't forget to ask children to suggest various ways to sort too.

Surprising Manipulatives

What do you get when you put a group of children together? Among other things, you get plenty of real, live manipulatives for great math activities! When children become their own props, there are an endless number of ways they can sort, pattern, measure, and count themselves!

Group time presents a wonderful opportunity for children to engage in math activities on a life-size scale. Also, the peer interaction of a group provides children with good models for participation and with opportunities to hear a wide spectrum of estimations and comparisons. This helps children begin to expand their own math ideas.

Asking "How are we the same?" and "How are we different?" is a great way to start a people-sorting activity. Children might begin by grouping themselves according to the color they are wearing. To extend the sorting activity, make a graph. Tape lines to the floor and above each line, and hang a picture of, for example, shoes with laces and shoes without. Have children line up on the tape under the appropriate picture. To show one-to-one correspondence, ask children to hold hands with someone across from them on the other line. Talk about which line has more.

Collaborating Using
Manipulatives

As children gather around containers filled with manipulatives, ideas instantly spark and merge. One child begins to line up small vehicles. Another suggests sorting them by color. Yet another offers to build a road for them with blocks.

Manipulatives help develop essential math concepts, and are a natural for inspiring children to work cooperatively. When children explore these materials as a group, they create their own ways to use them and construct their own learning together.

Manipulatives help make mathematical concepts easy and fun. As children experiment together, they try out new ideas.

Organizational Tips

The trick to handling little pieces in a large space is to be organized. The following tips can help.

■ **Clearly mark containers** so that all materials have a place. This makes children more likely to return them.

■ **Prepare all your materials in advance.** This will eliminate the need to get up and leave the group. (And we all know what a group likes to do when left alone!)

■ **Provide small trays, place mats, or rugs** for children to work in defined areas. When they work on the floor, it's often difficult for them to see where their materials are.

■ **Create a distinct signal** to regain children's attention. A few bangs on a drum or three claps will let them know it's the end of exploration time and the beginning of cleanup time.

Time for Observing

The skills children develop by participating in large-group activities with math manipulatives build a foundation for future learning. They often follow a simple equation: exploration + observation + more exploration = learning.

Children aren't the only ones who learn from using manipulatives together. Another advantage to setting up these materials at group time is that you can gain knowledge about children's developing math skills. The children are together in one place where you can quickly observe and assess which math-related skills they may need help with, how they're doing with particular math concepts, and how they solve problems with one another.

Making Manipulatives Work

Here are a few ways to use math materials to enrich group learning opportunities:

Pique children's interest. You might try hiding objects in a bag or box, then giving clues about what the items look or feel like. Once the mystery is solved, encourage children to suggest ways to use the materials. The group discussion is bound to generate ideas that even you might not have thought of.

Let children explore freely. Try putting a container filled with colored plastic links in the center of your circle and letting children investigate different ways to use the materials for a few minutes. This is also a great time for you to jot down some observations.

Encourage children to share ideas. It's important for children to learn about each other's thinking. But it may be difficult for some children to explain their thoughts, especially if a mathematical concept is new to them. You can be on hand to provide them with the vocabulary words they might need.

Offer your suggestions. After children have shared their ideas, you can help develop them and present new ones too. For example, if children are creating a red, blue, yellow, and green pattern with plastic links, you might suggest that they compare it with other patterns around the room or use it as a measuring tool.

Make connections to the math center. Using manipulatives at group time can offer new learning experiences. But be sure to make them available every day for children to explore independently and cooperatively at other times as well. They'll use their group experiences as a springboard to higher and higher levels of exploration and problem solving that they can then report on at your next group time.

Measuring, Graphing & Estimating

 few children are sitting on the floor in the block corner, surrounded by blocks and toy trucks. Suddenly Sara says, "Let's see how may trucks long I am!" She lies on the floor as the others place a row of trucks alongside her, head to toe, and everybody counts to see just how many trucks it takes to measure her. The children's spontaneous activity has become a wonderful math exploration!

Measuring

It's important to offer children math-related activities that grow from their own experiences. For example, try inviting children to use a piece of ribbon or a strip of construction paper to measure their height or the length of their arms. Remember to repeatedly use phrases such as "as long as," "the same as," "longer (or shorter) than." These phrases become a basic framework as children adopt the language of math in their everyday conversation.

Graphing

Young children enjoy graphing activities when they are about real things, such as laced and slip-on shoes, different-colored socks, or blocks of various sizes.

First, children need plenty of experience comparing the real objects before they can understand symbolic representation in a picture graph. Next, try making a pictorial graph using pictures to represent the object or events you're comparing. Help children see that the purpose of making graphs is to make concrete comparisons.

Estimating

Young children are often wild guessers when they first begin to estimate amounts. With successive experiences they make closer and closer approximations. (and this is what's important — not the right answer).

When designing an estimating event, limit the number of items to the range your children are familiar with. To begin, place five or six items in a plastic bag, and ask children to estimate how many are in the bag without counting.

Most important: Keep it light and fun! When taking a walk outside, ask children to estimate how many steps it will take them to get to a tree, then try it out. Next, ask if it would take more or fewer steps if they walked in giant steps! Baby steps! Backwards! Twirls!

Long-Term Projects

Long-term projects like surveys can be a fun way to involve everyone. Do them in small groups, then share your results. Small groups can each take a topic, such as eye or hair color, shoes, or pets. Survey the entire group, and graph their results.

Whatever activities you choose to do, remember to keep materials available for children to use in their own ways so they can apply mathematical thinking in their everyday activities. Children will begin to see that math isn't just something you learn about, but something that's a part of life!

Final note: Measuring, graphing, and estimating are usually thought of as teacher-initiated, whole-group activities, yet they can also arise spontaneously from children's play. As a general rule, whole-group experiences that actively involve everyone work best. Collaborate with children to brainstorm contributing roles for all.

Literature & Math

There are many wonderful storybooks that deal with mathematical concepts. Try one of these to introduce a topic in a large-group setting:

Anno's Counting Book by Mitsumasa Anno (Philomel Books)

Benjamin Budge and Barnaby Ball by Florence Parry Heide (Scholastic)

Count and See by Tana Hoban (Macmillan)

Eating Fractions by Bruce McMillan (Scholastic)

Inch by Inch by Leo Lionni (Astor)

Miss Spider's Teaparty by David Kirk (Scholastic)

One More and One Less by Guilio Maestro (Crown)

One, Two, Three by Brian Wildsmith (Franklin Watts)

The Very Hungry Caterpillar by Eric Carle (Philomel)

Solving Problems

When children work together to recognize problems and come up with solutions, they begin to realize that what they do can make a difference. Problem solving is an important group activity because it encourages children to think on their own, listen to the suggestions of others, weigh the validity of their own hypotheses as well as those brought up by the group, and come up with new ideas. Problem solving is a process of identifying a problem or a goal, generating ideas to solve or reach it, then testing the ideas. Through this process children also develop a sense of group — an ability to work as contributing members.

Problem-Solving Tips

■ **Ask your children** how they would handle it. Children will be able to participate in solving the problem as well as see the results of their thinking.

■ **Avoid jumping in to solve problems** too quickly yourself. That's not always easy to do when spontaneous events are happening quickly!

■ **Invite suggestions from everyone.** If your group can't think of enough suggestions, ask ancillary staff to help.

■ **Experiment with solutions** — and take your time doing it. You may be surprised to find out something really does work!

■ **Share the results.** Children, like adults, need to be recognized for their problem solving efforts!

Problem Solving at Group Time

There are two forms of problem solving: creative thinking, as demonstrated above, and social problem solving, dealing with natural problems or conflicts that occur in the classroom and in everyday life. These might include overcrowding at the water table, taking turns with swings, or sharing a new toy. When you involve children in the process of solving these problems at group time, you show them that you value their opinions and want to use their ideas to improve the situation.

In both forms of problem solving, children use essential thinking and language skills that are the basis of intellectual, creative, and social development. In the process, they gain self-esteem and are empowered to eventually work out the larger issues in their lives.

Seize the Moment

As you look for opportunities to invite children to solve problems, keep in mind their natural ability to notice problems. Take note of their observations and listen to their questions. Here is one example:

During free play, a few children discover that a favorite puzzle is missing a piece, so they bring the puzzle to you. Rather than saying "Thank you. I'll see what I can do," you ask them to think of ways the puzzle could be fixed. One child suggests making a new piece. Together, you learn to use wood putty, trace a pattern, and make the new piece. And the children paint it themselves! Problem solving provides a focus for group time activities, especially for kindergartners. It's a way to introduce children to the work of creative and critical thinking — both as individuals and as part of a group. By brainstorming many ways to solve a problem, children break away from conventional thinking and begin to see the endless possibilities the mind can create. Later, the teacher might offer children more concrete experience with the brainstorming process, by inviting the children to experiment with their ideas in the art, science, or block areas.

Help the Process

Here are several steps to guide children through a problem-solving process, though not every problem has a definite solution.

Define the problem. By asking open-ended questions that encourage children to talk about what

Books to Try

Cloudy With a Chance of Meatballs by Judi Barrett (Atheneum)

Company's Coming by Arthur Yorinks (Scholastic)

Grandfather Twilight by Barbara Berger (Philomel)

Swimmy by Leo Lionni (Pantheon)

There Is a Nightmare in My Closet by Mercer Mayer (Dial)

they're doing, thinking, or feeling, you help children identify problems. If children can't verbalize the problem clearly, help them find a few key words and build from there.

Brainstorm solutions. Instead of finding one right answer to a question or problem, it's important for children to think of several options. By asking open-ended questions such as "What's another way you can do this?" or "What would happen if we tried this a different way?" you invite children to expand their thinking. Remember that brainstorming is the time for coming up with, not evaluating, many possible solutions. Let chil-

dren know that you welcome all their ideas. Accept all their ideas equally — avoid responding more enthusiastically to some ideas than to others.

Decide where to start. After brainstorming, children can choose, as a group, which ideas to test out. It's important to remember that problem solving is a fluid process. Children often think of one thing to try, then reshape it, modify it, or abandon it altogether to try something new. It's not necessary for them to stick to their original plan.

Select or create tools. Help children decide what they will need in order to try out their solutions. Let them know they are free to use materials in the room in usual

or unconventional ways. For example, fabric scraps can be used to make a collage and also for plugging a hole in a water tube. If the problem is a conflict between people, remind children that words are usually the best tools to use.

Experiment with solutions. Children need an encouraging climate for hands-on experimentation with the ideas they brainstorm at group time. Even if their idea makes a mess, or is a solution you think won't work, the learning and sense of independence that children gain from testing it are well worth the effort. By acknowledging all their ideas and experiments, you are reinforcing the idea that problem solving is a process.

Problem solving keeps group time child-centered and interactive, and it encourages cooperation. Children learn to hear and support each other's ideas, no matter how "odd" they may sound. Remember: It's not the product of the problem-solving discussion that's important, but the process of thinking and experimenting that children go through.

Playing With Patterns

Patterns are everywhere. A true pattern, unlike other designs, repeats itself in a predictable manner. Most math concepts also fit a predictable pattern. When children become aware of patterns and how to use them, they gain an important problem-solving tool. Beginning patterns are simple. They usually involve only two variables or objects in a repetitive left-to-right line formation.

Children grasp the idea of patterns when they are given the opportunity to recognize and verbalize them. Preschoolers understand patterns best when repeating similar patterns using a variety of manipulatives.

Stories With Patterns

Here are a few predictable pattern stories:

Ask Mr. Bear by Marjorie Flack (Macmillan)

Blue Bug's Treasure by Virginia Poulet (Children's Press)

Brown Bear, Brown Bear by Bill Martin (Holt, Rinehart & Winston)

Chicken Soup With Rice by Maurice Sendak (Harper & Row)

The House That Jack Built by William Stobbs (Oxford University Press)

I Know an Old Lady by Rose Bonne and Graboff Abner (Scholastic)

The Little Circle by Ann Atwood (Charles Scribner's Sons)

Things to See: A Child's World of Familiar Objects by Tom Matthiesen (Platt)

Tikki, Tikki, Tembo by Arlene Mosel (Scholastic)

Introducing Patterns

Start with clear patterns. Use blocks, cut-out shapes, or colors to form a simple A-B-A-B line pattern. Put out the appropriate pieces to illustrate the pattern. Ask children, "What would come next in the pattern?"

People Patterns

Create a pattern formation with children. The easiest pattern to start with is "stand up — sit down." Organize children in a line, alternately standing and sitting. Have each child verbalize his part of the pattern by saying his position ("Standing!" "Sitting!").

Clap and Stamp a Pattern

Auditory skills enhance children's understanding of patterns. Try accompanying patterns with clapping and stomping sounds. For example, use a clap for "stand up" and a stamp for "sit down" as children say the "stand/sit" pattern.

Sing and Clap a Pattern

Language offers limitless ways to build and express patterns. Try this song to help children make up their own stomping and clapping patterns:

The Pattern Song
(Tune: "If You're Happy and You Know It")

Put your two feet on the ground
and stomp like me
(Stomp, stomp)

Put your two feet on the ground
and stomp like me
(Stomp, stomp)

Put your two feet on the ground
And stomp them up and down
Put your two feet on the ground
and stomp like me.
(Stomp, stomp)

Make Shoe Patterns

Invite children to participate in this pattern-making activity. While they sit in a group, ask children to remove one of their shoes. Begin an A-B-A-B pattern line in the center of the group with your shoe. Alternate each shoe in a sole-up, sole-down pattern. Invite children to take turns placing their shoes in the pattern. Now say the pattern together. Try two soles up, one sole down, two soles up, one sole down. Now say that pattern aloud. Encourage and try pattern suggestions from children.

Patterns All Around

Bring a variety of items that have patterns to school. Include clothing with stripes or checks, woven gloves, scarves, blankets, wallpaper, wrapping paper, beads, and bracelets. Can children find the pattern on each item? Ask, "How are these patterns the same? How are they different?" Take a walk around your room or building to find patterns on the walls, curtains, and on other people's clothes.

SCIENCE
&
GROUP TIME

Cooperative explorations of the natural and physical
world broaden our circle to bring the outside in and the inside out.
By investigating science phenomena together,
children benefit from one another's insights and observations.

Predicting Together

"What do you think will happen when we put this leaf in the water? Do you think this tiny pebble can float? How about this piece of construction paper?" There is a feeling of anticipation and excitement as children gather around the tub of water. You've already recorded each of their predictions on an experience/prediction chart. Now they will take turns testing them out by placing each object in the water. There are cheers and sighs as they watch what happens.

Learning centers are often the place where science exploration takes place. During group time, children can get together and share observations and ideas.

All Set for Science

When a science experiment is organized as a group time activity, you can make sure all your children gain a basic understanding of the concept and begin to see how their thinking relates to others'. The secret is to prepare the experiment in such a way that everyone can participate without getting bored or frustrated.

The following suggestions will help you facilitate science learning at group time.

Be prepared. Collect all of the materials you'll need, and arrange them in the area where they'll be used. Decide which ones you want children to focus on first, and make sure only those are in view. Keep other materials in a bag or box, close by but out of sight. (If you have too many things out, children will feel confused and get distracted.)

Organize your space so that everyone can see. Try making a low work table out of hollow blocks. This will keep the experiment off the floor but not too high for children to see. Ask everyone to gather in a horseshoe around the table, and place a prediction chart behind you.

Have your prediction chart ready. Set up your chart ahead of time so children can concentrate on the activity and their predictions. Make two columns on the chart: one for children's predictions and one for the results. For example, when you do the "What Can You Blow Away?" experiment, write the question at the top, then list the items you are testing down the side of the page. Tape a real item or a picture next to each word. Then make two columns running down the page. At the top, label one "Predictions" and the other "Results." Divide each column into a "Yes" and a "No" column large enough for children to make their own tally marks in the appropriate place.

Involve everyone. Ask open-ended questions that invite children to give their opinions. Have enough supplies so that each child has a chance to participate.

Keep things moving! These experiences can drag on if too much time is spent on one aspect. Move quickly but without rushing. Don't ask too many questions or try to "teach" the concept. Instead, think of this time as an opportunity to give children a taste of the concept. Their depth of understanding will grow later, in small-group settings, at their own develmental levels.

Make comparisons together. At the end of the activity, help childen compare their predictions with the results. Encourage them to comment on the experience.

Simple Science

Use each of these science questions as a title in a prediction chart when you do other simple experiments:

- **What objects** will light shine through?
- **What floats?** What sinks?
- **What materials** absorb water?
- **What will happen if** we mix these colors?
- **What objects** are attracted to magnets?
- **What happens when we mix** different liquids with water?
- **What happens when we roll** a ball down different kinds of ramps?
- **How much** water will we have when we melt this snow?
- **How small** will this puddle be tomorrow?
- **How long will it take** for the bulb to sprout?
- **What will happen to** my shadow at noon?
- **How long will it take** for the dripping faucet to fill a cup?

Exploring & Questioning

What's in the bag?" asks the teacher, holding up a plastic sandwich bag. "Nothing!" the children emphatically reply. The teacher waves the bag through the air, seals it, and asks, "Now what is in the bag?" Looking a little confused, some children still say, "Nothing," while others begin to wonder.

Exploring a New Concept

Air is a tricky and exciting science concept to bring to group time — tricky because it's not something children can see, and exciting because there are so many ways children experience the effects of air and wind daily.

This teacher used a sandwich bag to introduce the concept of air. She invited the children to touch the sealed bag, then asked, "Does it feel different from a flat bag?" Children began to realize that there must be something inside — they could feel it! After experimenting with their own bags, the group decided that air must be inside the bag.

Using Group Time to Probe the Concept

When introducing a science concept at group time, start with a simple experiment that encourages children to tap into their own knowledge. Invite them to share their thoughts with the rest of the class. The children in this class exchanged ideas about where air is found and how it can be used.

Ask children what they would like to learn next. Because of her children's curiosity, this teacher asked, "What else would you like to find out about air and wind?"

Asking Questions

Is air everywhere? How do people use air or wind? This teacher recorded children's questions to use as the basis for explorations at the next group meeting and to create learning-center activities and additional research projects.

Group meetings encourage cooperative, creative, and critical thinking by children. They learn to listen to one another's ideas, to take turns making suggestions, and to explore a science concept as a group. They practice important self-expression skills and develop self-esteem as they begin to see themselves as essential partners in developing class curriculum.

What's Next?

Where you go from here depends upon your class, but here are a few suggestions:

Encourage active exploration. At the next group time, the children in this class decided to investigate how air feels and moves. The teacher invited them to reach out and "touch" the air and to move it with their bodies. Children discovered they had to move the air to feel it.

One child wondered how she could see the effect of air. The teacher invited the children to sit in a circle holding the edge of a parachute. Then they all jumped up in unison and watched the air inflate the parachute.

Use the outdoors. The outdoors offers many opportunities for air exploration. This class took their parachute outside and experimented to see the effect of wind on it. They played with streamers and kites to see which way the wind was blowing.

Record children's findings. After enjoying many experiences with air and wind, the children returned to group time to record their findings on a chart titled "What We Learned About Air."

Air-Related Stories

Set the stage for further exploration with these books:

Air by Chris Oxlade (Barron's Educational Series, Inc.)

Air by Angela Webb (Franklin Watts Inc.)

Air & Flight by Barbara Taylor (Franklin Watts Inc.)

Air Is All Around You by Franklyn M. Branley (HarperCollins)

Curious George Flies a Kite by Margaret Rey (Houghton Mifflin)

In the Air by Henry Pluckrose (Children's Press)

Play With the Wind by Howard E. Smith, Jr. (McGraw-Hill)

The Wind Blew by Pat Hutchins (Penguin)

When the Wind Stops by Charlotte Zolotow (Harper & Row)

Discovering
Through the Five Senses

What happens when you bring out a new toy or art material to use? Children immediately want to see it, touch it, and shake it. And if you're working with prekindergartners, they may want to taste it as well. It is through the senses that children gain information, interpret it, make comparisons and predictions, and then draw conclusions.

You can provide children with many opportunities to explore and play using their five senses.

Sense-able Books

Try these books with your children:

TOUCH

Mary Ann's Mud Day by Janice M. Udry (Harper & Row)

My Bunny Feels Soft by Charlotte Steiner (Knopf)

HEARING

A Crowd Full of Cows by John Graham (Scholastic)

Too Much Noise by Ann McGovern (Scholastic)

SIGHT

I Spy by Jean Marzollo (Scholastic-Cartwheel)

Spectacles by Ellen Raskin (Macmillan)

TASTE

Miss Pennypuffer's Taste Collection by Louise B. Scott (McGraw-Hill)

The Very Hungry Caterpillar by Eric Carle (Putnam)

SMELL

Benny's Nose by Mel Cebulash (Scholastic)

Follow Your Nose by Paul Showers (Thomas Y. Crowell)

Touch and Tell

Children grasp new concepts through touch. Touching activities are more than fun; they help young children learn in the way they understand best.

Explore. Our bodies and the clothes we wear are covered with many different textures. Ask children to explore the different textures on themselves. Guide the group from head to toe, exploring how their hair, eyelashes, nose, mouth, shirt, pants, and shoes feel. Encourage children to use descriptive language as they explore.

Play. Hold a tactile show-and-tell. Ask children to bring something from home they think is interesting to touch, and hide it in a paper bag. Before you hold your show-and-tell, talk about words such as *smooth, bumpy, soft, hard, warm, cold,* and *squishy.* Then invite children, one at a time, to use descriptive words to give clues about what their object is. Each child can place his or her object under a cloth so classmates can touch and try to identify it.

Listen to This

Children are keenly aware of the sounds around them, even though it doesn't always seem that way. Sometimes children need time to process what they hear. So you may find them referring to an event, a strange noise, or a read-aloud story long after it has occurred.

Observe. A great way to focus on the sense of hearing is to sit and listen. Ask children to close their eyes for a minute and quietly listen for any sounds around them. It may take a few tries for them to notice the subtle sounds of the room, the outdoors, and their bodies.

Ask children to sit quietly as you tape-record the "silence." Play back the tape. Is it really silent?

Play. Introduce a "Where Are You?" circle game, which will help children locate the direction that a sound is coming from.

Choose two children to stand in the center of a large circle. Loosely blindfold the child who chooses to be "It." Then ask the other child to move quietly around the inside of the circle. When "It" asks, "Where are you?" the other child stops and says, "Here I am!" and stands still. Then "It" moves toward the source of the sound. Remove the blindfold to let the children see how close to each other they are standing.

Look Again

Young children are constantly using their eyes to observe and interpret information.

Observe. Before group time, change a few things about your clothing and appearance, and see whether children notice. For example, you might change your hair, wear two different earrings, or wear a pin upside down. Then begin group time as usual. If children don't mention anything, ask them if they notice something unusual about you this morning.

Explore. Place between three and five items on a tray, and invite children to look carefully at everything there. You might ask them to name each item. Then, while children have their eyes closed, remove one item. Ask, "What's missing?"

Just a Taste

Children feel more comfortable experimenting with new tastes when they see others sample new foods.

Observe. Have a group time tasting party. Bring in a new food for children to explore and taste, such as an unusual fresh or dried fruit or vegetable.

Play. Organize a taste-test game. Collect a variety of foods for children to taste. You might choose foods based on themes, such as corn products (fresh, frozen, or canned corn, corn flakes, corn syrup). Include a discussion of things that should never be tasted. Introduce the frown-face symbol of "Mr. Yuk" on things that are not safe to taste.

The Nose Knows

Even though the sense of smell is one of the more delicate senses, it's still one that children use fully.

Observe. Bring in items with a variety of odors: scented candles, soaps, spices, perfumes, dryer sheets, pine branches, and flowers. Pass the items around for children to investigate. Then ask children to take turns sorting the items into piles according to smells they like and don't like.

Play. Make a smell-matching game by filling pairs of small containers with spices, extracts, toothpaste, aftershave, and so on. Cover the containers so children can't see what's inside. Then ask them to find the two containers that match and identify what's inside.

Our Five Senses

	To Taste	To Smell	To Touch	To Hear	To See
What we like	Ice Cream Cheese	Flowers	Kittens Clay Bubbles	Saxophone	The Moon Fireworks
What we don't like	Pickles	Tar Garbage		Fireworks	Blood

Today's Weather:

Observing
How We Grow

n all areas of development — social, emotional, cognitive, language, and physical — everyone is always changing. Anytime can be a time to celebrate the growth of the entire group and of each child, as well.

Open a discussion about children's successes. You might ask, "Who can tell me what you can do now that you couldn't do before?" Start an "I Can" chart of their ideas, and invite each child to contribute at least one thing to the chart. If children need help getting started, suggest that they think about the different centers in the room or the different parts of the day.

Celebrate Social and Emotional Growth

This is an area of significant change for young children, especially in their ability to work cooperatively. Most likely, a sense of family has been growing in your room, and members of the family can celebrate together. Friendship, sharing, and talking through problems can be discussed.

Celebrate Language Growth

Young children's language development is another area of great growth. You've probably noticed that some children who were hardly willing to speak at the beginning of the year are now giving long speeches at group time.

Make a group yearbook together. Invite children to draw a self-portrait, leaving room where they can dictate or write something about themselves. You might suggest that they tell what they learned or what they liked best this year.

Remember to draw your own picture and write something about yourself too. Make photocopies of the pages, and make a book for each child.

Celebrate Cognitive Growth

Ask children to suggest things that they know about, and make a chart of their abilities. Some may be proud that they know their name and age, while others may celebrate knowing the alphabet song, their phone number, how to count to 10, or their colors. It's important to acknowledge these skills, but it's also important to help children see that they've developed problem-solving, hypothesizing, and predicting skills, too.

Celebrate Physical Development

In many ways, children are proudest of their physical growth and change. It's so obvious to them—they've gotten taller, they can walk down the stairs one at a time, they can throw and catch a ball. To help children show off their growth, invite them to bring to school one article of clothing that they've outgrown this year. Your group time will likely be filled with giggles as children share their too-small shirts, sweaters, or sneakers.

Why not take group time outdoors to celebrate physical growth? Consider holding an Olympics, and set up a variety of noncompetitive games. Give each child an award for participating.

As you try these activities, remember that some children have grown and changed more than others, but all need to be supported.

Year-long Celebration

To help young children think about their accomplishments, discuss favorites over the year at group time. Write headings on an experience chart. You might try:

- Songs We Love
- Things We Made
- Books We Liked
- Places We Went

■ **Illustrate the experience chart** with photos or drawings of favorite activities.

■ **Close your discussion** by reading back through the lists on the experience chart.

■ **Ask children to vote** on their favorite items in each category.

■ **Celebrate** by singing their favorite song and reading their favorite book.

MOVEMENT, MUSIC
& Group Time

*Every shared music and movement experience is a chance
for children to express feelings and unite in the power
of rhythm and song. Music also provides new ways to learn
about the world and develop a myriad of skills.*

Fun With Rhythm

We are surrounded by rhythm — the seasons of the year, the cycle of day and night, the beating of our own hearts. The basic rhythm of life pervades our waking and sleeping hours, and children acquire rhythm and movement skills quite naturally.

Where to Begin

Rhythmic-movement activities at group time can come from many sources. Why not start with children's bodies? If available, provide a stethoscope so children can listen to their own heartbeats. Encourage them to tap out the rhythm they hear and feel inside. Invite children to keep the rhythm going and create a movement to go with it.

Counting in Time

Rhythmic-movement activities provide excellent opportunities to practice counting with purpose. Have children clap as you count "One, two, three." Then ask them to think of movements they can do three times: wave three times, tap three times, wiggle their noses three times. Graduate to larger movements — steps, jumps, spins, or shakes. Invite children to create a three-part movement and freeze on the last part. Then ask them to look around the group to see the interesting "sculptures" they created.

Fingerplay Fun

Fingerplays invite children to use their fingers and hands to interpret a song or a chant. Even by moving just their fingers, they use up some of the tension stored inside their bodies. Look for ways to keep fingerplays open-ended. You might start by asking "How many different ways can you think of to move your fingers?"

Or you can use traditional or favorite fingerplays and invite children to invent adaptations of them. "Open, Shut Them," a chant about moving hands, grabs children's attention and provides just the right amount of silliness:

Open, shut them, open, shut them.
Give a great big clap.
Open, shut them, open, shut them.
Put them in your lap.
Creep them, creep them,
*   creep them, creep them,*
Right up to your chin.
Open up your little mouth, but …
Do not let them in!

Walk to the Beat

Here are some walking games that can help children explore their own walking rhythms:

■ **Invite children to clap with each step.** (You may notice that they will eventually start clapping and stepping in unison.)

■ **Slow down or speed up** the beat of the clap; children will modify their walking to fit the rhythm.

■ **Ask children to walk and clap** to the rhythm of their names. First, ask children to say their names and clap on each syllable. Next, invite them to walk it as they say it: "Jes-si-ca, Jes-si-ca." Finally, invite children to try walking to the rhythm of one another's names.

Action-Rhyme Adventures

Part of the excitement of action rhymes comes from using the body to express emotions. Some rhymes encourage children to feel capable by inviting them to act out skills or accomplishments. Other rhymes provide children with safe ways to act out and overcome fear or danger. As you know, children sometimes feel small in comparison to the objects and adults around them. "The Turtle" is one rhyme that invites them to feel big and brave:

There was a little turtle that
lived on a rock.
He swam in the water and
climbed on a rock.
He snapped at a mosquito,
he snapped at a flea,
He snapped at a minnow,
and he snapped at me.
He caught the mosquito,
he caught the flea,
He caught the minnow,
but he can't catch me!

Another fun and exciting action rhyme is the classic "We're Going on a Bear (or Lion) Hunt." In this rhyme, children use their hands and voices to make the motions and sounds of walking through grass, crossing a bridge, swimming across a river, and climbing a tree as they search for a scary bear. When they finally meet him sitting high in the tree, children use the same motions to pretend to race back past the river, bridge, and grass until they arrive safely — and often breathlessly — home!

Relaxation Exercises

Sometimes what's needed in February is an opportunity for calm, centered movements. Quiet breathing and slow-motion exercises can be a source of fun and creative expression. At the same time, these movements help children release tension and become aware of their bodies in new ways.

A relaxing way for children to exercise large muscles is to breathe slowly while they form their bodies into the shapes or positions of objects or animals. When you introduce this activity, talk in a soft voice and encourage children to move slowly and quietly. Once they interpret the object or animal in their own ways, suggest that they hold the positions while continuing to breathe slowly.

The Tree: Together, think about different trees you've seen. Then stand up straight and raise your arms to look like a tree. Breathe slowly in and out, and try to hold the pose for about 30 seconds.

The Cat: Find a comfortable way to curl up like a cat and pretend to be sleeping in a warm, relaxing place, such as near a fireplace or on a sunny windowsill. Then wake up and stretch.

The Turtle: Pretend to be a turtle by curling your back like a shell and tucking your head, arms, and legs underneath. Hold the pose and breathe. Then, very slowly, stretch out your neck, arms, and legs.

Remember, rhythm is everywhere. As you move through your day with children, point out and reinforce the rhythm of their movements in everything they do. Your children will be exploring important math concepts, gaining an awareness of their bodies, and exploring new ways to express their feelings all at once!

There's Music in Me

Songs are magical tools that help children listen and participate more fully during circle time. They can introduce concepts, reinforce and develop language skills, encourage self-expression, and foster growth in motor skills.

Music also helps children feel and experience rhythm. When children are exposed to a variety of musical sounds and songs, they learn to appreciate many different beats and, at the same time, become familiar with important cultural traditions.

Great Recordings

Try any or all of these wonderful instrumental recordings.

Classical:

The Carnival of the Animals by Camille Saint Saens

The Classical Child: Volumes One and Two by Metro Music

The Nutcracker Suite by Pyotr Ilyich Tchaikovsky

Pictures at an Exhibition by Modest Moussorgsky

Jazz and New Age:

Between the Worlds by Patrick O'Hearn (Private Music)

Chameleon Days by Yanni (Private Music)

Nightnoise by Bill Oskay and Michael O'Domhnaill (Windham Hill)

Silk Road by Kitaro (Geffen)

White Winds by Andreas Vollenweider (CBS)

Music Means Fun!

Whether you're listening to the soulful tune of a big bass violin, marching to the colorful rat-a-tat-tat of snare drums, or singing and clapping together to a favorite song, music has a special appeal that is hard to resist. Join in — there's a song in your setting that's just waiting to be sung!

Music That Sings

Teaching a song to a group of young children takes a little bit of talent and some good old-fashioned know-how. Here are some easy-to-follow guidelines to help you along:

Introduce songs in a relaxed, comfortable manner. Remember, children need to sing just for the fun of it without pressure to participate or to perform perfectly.

Use props. Gather objects such as puppets and photographs to help you illustrate what the song is about.

Briefly explain the song. Talk to children about where the song comes from, how much you have enjoyed it, and what it relates to in their experiences.

Enjoy yourself. Make sure you've memorized the song so you don't have to look at the music. Use lots of facial expressions and hand gestures. Smile while you sing!

Take your time. Introduce each song by singing it without accompaniment. (It's easier for children to hear the words.) Sing the song slowly (but not too slowly) straight through to the end. Enunciate clearly and make eye contact. Repeat the song several times, and invite children to join in when they feel comfortable. If possible, use hand motions for children to imitate.

Continue to incorporate the song into your day. Sing it spontaneously and repeat it frequently over the next few days and weeks. Be careful not to introduce too many new songs at a time. Children love to sing familiar songs over and over again.

Strike Up the Band!

Rhythm instruments will captivate and teach your children about the power and magic of music.

To enable children to get the most out of rhythm instruments, it

is necessary to do two things. First, point out that classroom instruments are not toys, but real instruments just like a piano, a violin, or a guitar. If children are taught from the beginning to respect the instruments, they will use them appropriately.

Second, it's important to introduce and use the instruments in an organized way. Introduce them one at a time — if possible, one a day. This way, children can focus on one specific instrument and the sound it makes. One day, pass out all of the rhythm sticks you have, and let children take turns making different sounds (if you don't have enough sticks for everyone, children can share).

When using rhythm instruments, avoid using melodic instruments such as xylophones. These instruments are meant to be used to play melodies. When they are played freely by children, these instruments will produce a loud, discordant sound uncoordinated to the melody. Try to use nonmelodic percussion instruments such as drums, tambourines, wood and sand blocks, triangles, rhythm sticks, maracas, and bells.

Music Around the World

Young children enjoy many different kinds of music, so don't hesitate to share a variety of styles and genres such as jazz, calypso, reggae, classical, folk, and rock. Use records and tapes to introduce the sounds of many kinds of instruments — congas, bongos, bells, maracas, saxophones, and harps. As you play music, encourage children to experience the rhythms by moving.

Share tapes and records like *Catherine Slonecki's Children's Songs Around the World* (Educational Activities, Inc., Freeport, NY). This music will expose children to a wide variety of songs from all over the world. Dance movements are also suggested. Enjoy moving together in a circle to the choruses, pantomiming the actions of the songs, and playing along with rhythm instruments.

Make Music With Me

Invite parents to participate in your music experiences. Send home a note asking them to think about songs that hold special cultural and family memories — songs they learned from their parents and grandparents when they were younger, instruments and music that are a part of their cultural heritage — that they would like to share with your group. When you know which parents would like to participate, decide whether to invite them to your program one at a time or all together for a music fest. After sharing their songs, family members can stay for an international snack. Teach children a song to sing to the group:

(Tune: "Ring Around the Rosie")

Music makes me sing,
Music makes me smile.
Sing along,
Sing along,
Sing along with me!

Feeling the Music

Young children are full of feelings, and music and movement are perfect outlets for expressing them. In the process of being something or someone else, children often lose their self-consciousness and feel free to just "be a feeling."

Everyone has feelings that need to be expressed. When you encourage these feeling activities, you are telling children that it is good to feel and that there are many ways to express feelings.

When you share your own feelings and accept and acknowledge the feelings of others, you are acting as a model for children.

A Song of Feelings

Sing the song "When I Feel Happy" to the tune of "Mulberry Bush."

When I Feel Happy

When I feel happy,
I clap my hands,
clap my hands,
clap my hands.
When I feel happy,
I clap my hands,
early in the morning.

Then ask, "How else can we show happiness while we sing this song? How can we show it with our whole bodies? With just our little fingers?" Sing the song again, using new motions. Then think of another emotion and ways to show it. Encourage children to use all parts of their bodies as they show their feelings.

Colorful Music

Talk about the ways music can make people feel: Some music sounds happy and might make you feel like spinning and leaping, and other music is sad and might make you feel like crawling.

Place a large sheet of mural paper on the floor with a variety of crayons and markers. Invite children to sit around the paper. Together, examine the colors of the crayons and markers. Talk about happy and sad colors. Then play parts of recordings that induce different moods. You might try Saint Saen's "Carnival of the Animals."

Help children choose colors that illustrate the way the music makes them feel. Then use the crayons and markers to "dance" on the paper. Encourage children to change the colors and their movements as the mood of the music changes.

Body Talk

Talk about the ways people can show feelings without using words. Ask children to think about how people look when they are happy, shy, and angry. Ask, "How can you make your body say, 'I'm happy!' or 'I'm scared'?" Take turns and vary the feelings. Then ask children to use their bodies to act out simple situations such as "Come here. I'm so glad to see you!" or "I need to be alone right now."

Now try body talk with "what if..." situations. Ask, "What if someone just gave you a puppy for your birthday? How would your body and face look?" or "What if your friend told you she didn't want to play with you anymore?" You might ask children to make up their own situations, feelings, and phrases to act out.

Happy Machines

Make a list of all the feelings children can think of. Say, "Pretend you are a machine that can show feelings. How would you move if you were a Happy Machine?" Play music that sounds mechanical, such as Hap Palmer's *Pretend* album. Invite children to move to the music like happy machines. Then encourage them to become sad, angry, and shy machines. Help them use their whole bodies to show what they are feeling.

Instruments and Feelings

Pass out rhythm instruments, and invite children to experiment with the different sounds. Ask which instruments make happy, sad, shy, spooky, and angry sounds. Use the instruments to accompany a favorite song, such as the one in the box or "If You're Happy and You Know It." Change the words to say "If you're happy and you know it, make a sound." Change the verse to indicate other emotions. Encourage children to also make up sounds. Eventually, you might even make up a dance.

GROUP TIME
& the World
OUTSIDE

Soften the walls of your classroom
by using group time as a bridge to people, places,
and things in the real world.

Welcoming Special Visitors

Inviting visitors to group time is a wonderful way to bring the outside world into your setting. Through visitors, children make new discoveries; they see, hear, and hopefully touch new things while remaining in their safe, secure, and familiar environment. Also, the guests you invite can add depth and dimension to subjects in a way that books and pictures cannot. Through thoughtful preparation with your guest and your group, you can make sure that everyone has a fun, productive, and educational experience.

Finding Guests

Here are some suggestions:

■ **Parents and other family members:** They can talk about their careers, hobbies, or interests.

■ **People with interesting occupations:** Particularly any fix-it person who can actually perform his or her task right in your room.

■ **People with interesting hobbies:** Painting, sculpting, knitting, and weaving are always a big hit with young children.

■ **People with animals:** Farmers, pet-sho owners, nature-center personnel, and pet owners all make great candidates.

■ **People with cultural interests:** Invite people from interesting cultural backgrounds to share photographs, foods, tools, clothing, music, and personal stories from their countries.

Family Visitors

Your classroom is an exciting mixture of many cultures and varied traditions. And elders — grandparents and great-grandparents — are our greatest resource for connecting children with the customs and observances of the past. Before movies, television, and video games, sitting around the fireplace with an elder and listening as he or she wove stories about the "old days" was a common family activity. History, culture, and family rituals were all shared through these oral communications.

You can continue this important tradition by inviting family members to share their varied experiences with your group. Interacting with older adults teaches children about the abundant wisdom, talent, and love elders possess. Children also learn to respect each other's different customs and ways of life.

As their rapport develops, exchanges between child and elder become shared treasures. After Samantha's grandfather visited the classroom, one of her classmates exclaimed, "Wow, he went to kindergarten too!"

How to Invite Your Visitors

Consider the following suggestions:

Create a file of volunteers. Send out an announcement asking parents, community members, and even older siblings if they have a hobby, job, or talent they would like to share with preschoolers. As positive responses come in, fill out index cards with the names of prospective visitors, their phone numbers, the times they are available, and a short note about what they would like to share. Contact the visitor ahead of time.

Then plan a short meeting or phone conversation to offer a few suggestions to help the visit run smoothly. Remind the guest to keep it short and to bring props for children to see and touch. Let them know that young children are visual learners who listen best when there is something to look at.

Asking simple questions that engage children in conversation makes the visit very effective. Suggest appropriate open-ended questions, such as "What do you think I do with this?" and "How do you think I made this?"

Prepare Your Children

Let children know that someone special is coming to visit. (With older preschoolers, you might mark the date on a calendar.) Talk

Handling the Excitement

Here are a few steps you can take to ensure that children have a productive experience:

■ **Talk to families in advance:** Explain the importance of involving their child in the visit.

■ **Ease the visitor's transition into the classroom:** Invite the visitor to come early so that the child has time for greetings.

■ **Make the child a part of the visit:** Ask the visitor to make the child a partner in the group time event by giving him or her a special job to do.

■ **Move beyond group time.** Involve the child in an activity with a relative.

about what the person does and what he will bring to share. List questions. As questions for and about the visitor come up, write them down together on a sheet of experience-chart paper.

Make predictions about the visitor. Encourage children to think about what the visitor will bring. For example, children might predict that a visiting doctor will be a man with a white coat who will give them shots, when actually you are expecting a woman who will let them listen to their hearts through a stethoscope. Talking about children's expectations will help you understand their fears and stereotypes and help you work through them.

Talk about behavior. Take time to reinforce appropriate circle time behaviors, such as taking turns to talk and sitting in their places.

Prepare the space. Children will love to help prepare your circle time area for a visitor. Before he arrives, move furniture around

so your guest will be comfortable and have plenty of room to show his props at children's eye level.

Remember, visitors are usually not as experienced with young children as you are. Be ready to help, if necessary, by asking questions and quietly reiterating limits. You might notice that a question needs to be phrased differently, a prop needs to be passed around so children can touch it, or the speaker needs to move on to another topic. Don't hesitate to enter into the presentation. Most speakers

willwelcome the help and children will stay turned in.

Share the Moment

When your visitor comes to group time, you may wish to sing a welcome song. This will be a good time for your guest to share whatever he or she has brought and for you and your children to ask questions from your experience chart. During this exchange, other questions are likely to arise. Children may be amazed to realize that some of their visitor's experiences are very similar to their own and others are quite different. This is a wonderful opportunity to value each person's uniqueness.

End on a positive note. Be sure to remind your guest when circle time is coming to an end (before children become distracted). It's always exciting if he can stay for activity time.

Keep in Touch

Between visits, children can draw pictures or write thank-you letters for their visitors. Perhaps children will receive a reply they can share at group time!

Let's Go Outside!

How about moving your group time outside today? First, you can provide children with opportunities to expand their thinking skills. Listen for comments like "This rock is heavier than our blocks!" or "This tree bark feels bumpy, like sandpaper." Second, taking group time outside develops children's attention skills. Children must focus on the activity and deal with outside "distractions" such as bird or traffic noises. Third, it is through their senses that children discover and explore.

Outdoor Tips

A little planning is all that's needed to take group time outdoors. Consider these points:

■ **Pick a place to explore**, and plan your activities accordingly.

■ **Select a comfortable place to meet.** Avoid areas that are too sunny or bumpy.

■ **Define boundaries.** Outside, children have a greater need to know what the limits of their meeting space are.

■ **Talk about rules.** Talk about outside safety, listening to and following directions carefully, and staying with the group.

■ **Keep activities simple.** When there is so much to see, hear, and touch, children can experience sensory overload and lose focus.

■ **Make the sessions active.** Do a limited amount of sitting and then move into more active learning.

Games and Activities

Here are some wonderful games and activities to make the most of your outdoor time together:

Do You Hear What I Hear? Take an old stethoscope outside and listen to quiet noises. Children are often amazed to hear sounds that come out of the ground, the sidewalk, and even trees. Experiment by making gentle noises on surfaces and listening to the differences.

Create a playground orchestra. Buildings, trees, play equipment, and rocks all make a variety of tones when struck with a drumstick. Make a musical fence by hanging pie tins, spoons, rattles, and other objects at children's level, and let them play away!

The Teeny, Tiny Sound. Invite children to hold hands and stand in a group with their feet slightly apart. Explain that you're going to tell them a little story that they can feel in their bodies, and ask them to drop hands and close their eyes. Then you might say, "Let's pretend that deep down inside your foot is a teeny, tiny sound. It's so quiet that you can hardly hear it. Listen inside and see if you can hear it. Now that sound is going to start slowly moving up your legs, and as it moves up your legs it's getting a teeny, tiny bit louder — loud enough that you may be able to hear it. In fact, you can make this tiny humming sound now.

"This sound is getting louder as it moves up to your knees and up to your stomach. It's getting even louder now. Can you make your hum louder? The sound is moving into your chest. The sound is getting louder and louder as it moves into your throat. The sound is about to jump out of your mouth with a big shout right now!"

Musical Carpets. Using carpet squares or towels, play a cooperative version of musical chairs. The object of this game is to help everyone find a place to sit; in other words, no one is ever "out." Ask children to arrange the carpet squares in a group and to stand outside the group. Then, as you beat a drum slowly, invite children to walk slowly around the group. When the drum stops, they sit on the nearest carpet square. After everyone has found a seat, ask children to stand up and remove about three carpet squares. Again, beat on the drum while they walk around the group. This time, when you stop, some children will need to share squares. Continue playing

Cooperative Games

Cooperative games develop positive feelings and build cooperation skills because everyone helps one another in order to win. Try these tips to encourage these benefits:

■ **Talk about rules,** reminding children that all the group time manners they use inside need to be used outside.

■ **Discuss the purpose** of taking group time outdoors. Explain that you have some new group games that work best when they're played outside.

■ **Introduce the concept** of cooperative games.

the game until all the children are piled together on just a few carpet squares.

The Knot. The first time you play this game, you might want to try it with four children at a time. Invite the other children to be a cheering squad for the participants and to offer suggestions. Ask the participants to stand in a group and to reach across it to hold hands with different children to make a knot. Then, while still holding hands, invite them to twist and turn and duck under arms to unravel the knot. With some luck and perseverance, they can unravel themselves back into a group.

A "Seeing" Treasure Hunt. Hide things around your play area in places where they blend in with the protective coloring of the environ-

ment. After children hunt for the objects, talk about how some animals have skin coverings that hide them outdoors. Ask children to hide themselves where their colors blend in too. You might also play an "I Spy" game, and just for fun, use spy glasses made of paper-towel tubes. The first player says, "I spy with my little eye something that has feathers and is sitting in a tree. Where is it?" The others use their spy glasses to find it.

Balloon Balance. Ask children to find a partner, and give each pair a balloon. Invite children to find different ways they can balance the balloon between them without using their hands! Once they have it balanced, ask them to try walking around the area without dropping the balloon. After children have done this for a while, beat a drum as a signal for them to try balancing the balloon a different way. Allow them to try different ways as long as they're interested.

Closing Time:
Rounding Out the Day

"Is it time to go home?"

"Can we read that story again tomorrow?"

"Look at my picture!"

A Song to End With

Sing a Song of Children
(tune: *"Sing a Song of Sixpence"*)
Sing a song of children
In our kindergarten.
We have many friends here,
Growing in our garden.
Filled with joyful smiles,
And names from A to Z,
Look around and you will see,
"We're as happy as can be!"

Closing time can be a period of reflection, one in which children gain a sense of closure by sharing the events of the day and discussing their feelings about them. Children use observation and evaluation skills as they take an active part in looking back at their day. By bringing children back into the circle of classroom community, you create a sense of family and support as children prepare to leave for home.

Invite children to review events and share personal accomplishments. Some may want to talk about what they have done, while others may want to show a project they have completed, such as a painting, book, or construction. Encourage children to share their feelings and ask questions of one another.

Encourage children to share their feelings. Discuss which activities they liked and disliked and which they would like to repeat or develop further tomorrow. Then create a "to do" list of their ideas. By inviting children to express their opinions, you help them gain a sense of partnership in the daily program and feel that their work and play have meaning and value.

Plan for tomorrow. Discussing upcoming events gives children the security of knowing what to expect and allows them to come to school prepared with ideas and materials from home.

Create a closing routine or ritual. By coming together again at the end of the day, you complete the circle started at the beginning. Some programs like to have children join hands in a circle and sing a song, say a poem, chant, or recite a class-written alma mater or pledge. Another possibility is to read a favorite story or a beginning-level chapter book with older children. They like the excitement of anticipating what will happen next in the story and look forward to that special time at the end of the day when everybody is back together to share the fun.

Whatever you choose to do during closing time, remember that each meeting weaves the threads of the day into a wonderful fabric of community; meeting time prepares children to leave your room feeling supported and connected to their school family.

Group Time Resources

These books will enhance your group times and will help foster explorations of a wide range of ideas and themes.

Learning & Growing With Group Time

Changes, Changes by Pat Hutchins (Simon & Schuster)

The Cleanup Surprise by Christine Loomis (Scholastic)

Going to Day Care by Fred Rogers (Putnam)

Jesse's Day Care by Amy Valens (Houghton Mifflin)

A New Day by Ronald Heunick (Gryphon House)

Getting to Know One Another

At the Stores by Colin McNaughton (Philomel Books)

A Chair for My Mother and *Something Special for Me* by Vera B. Williams (William Morrow & Co.)

Friday Night Is Papa's Night by Ruth Sonneborn (Puffin)

Let's Find Out About the Community by Valerie Pitt (Franklin Watts)

A Walk in the Neighborhood by June Behrens (Children's Press)

Creativity Around the Circle

Daydreamers by Eloise Greenfield (Dial Books)

Frederick by Leo Lionni (Alfred A. Knopf)

I Wish I Had a Computer That Makes Waffles by Fitzburgh Dodson (Oak Tree Publications)

Oh, Were They Ever Happy by Peter Spier (Doubleday)

The Scribble Monster by Jack Kent (Harcourt Brace Jovanovich)

Starbright by Maureen Garth (HarperCollins)

Literacy & Group Time

Animalia by Graeme Bose (Abrams)

Brown Bear, Brown Bear, What Do You See? by Bill Martin, Jr. (Holt)

Chicka Chicka Boom Boom by Bill Martin (Holt)

Eating the Alphabet by Lois Ehlert (Harcourt Brace)

Goodnight Moon by Margaret Wise Brown (HarperCollins)

Twenty-Six Letters and Ninety-Nine Cents by Tana Hoban (Greenwillow)

The Magic Fish by Freya Littledale (Scholastic)

Math & Group Time

Ask Mr. Bear by Marjorie Flack (Macmillan)

Bigger and Smaller by Robert Froman (HarperCollins)

Chicken Soup With Rice by Maurice Sendak (HarperCollins)

Jim and the Beanstalk by Raymond Briggs (Putnam)

The Line Up Book by Marisabina Russo (Greenwillow Books)

Science & Group Time

Everybody Needs a Rock by Byrd Baylor (Simon & Schuster)

Find Out by Touching by Paul Showers (HarperCollins)

Fingers Are Always Bringing Me News by Mary O'Neill (Doubleday)

Mud, Mud, Mud by Lenore Klein (Alfred A. Knopf)

Pat the Bunny by Dorothy Kunhardt (Western Pub. Co)

Touching for Telling by Illa Podendorf (Children's Press)

When Is Tomorrow? by Nancy Dingman Wilson (Alfred Knopf)

Movement, Music & Group Time

Caps for Sale by Esphyr Slobodkina (HarperCollins)

Hickory Dickory Dock and Humpty Dumpty by James Dunbar (Creative Edge)

Hush Little Baby by Aliki (Prentice-Hall)

Old MacDonald Had a Farm by Abner Graboff (Scholastic)

Quick as a Cricket by Audrey and Don Wood (Child's Play)

Six Little Ducks by Chris Conover (HarperCollins)

Skip to My Lou by Nadine Bernard Westcott (Little, Brown)